LINDENMEIER:
A PLEISTOCENE
HUNTING
SOCIETY

HARPER'S CASE STUDIES IN ARCHAEOLOGY

William A. Longacre,
General Editor

LINDENMEIER: A PLEISTOCENE HUNTING SOCIETY

EDWIN N. WILMSEN

Museum of Anthropology
University of Michigan

HARPER & ROW, PUBLISHERS
New York, Evanston, San Francisco, London

Cover photo: Courtesy of The American Museum of
Natural History.

Sponsoring Editor: Walter H. Lippincott, Jr.
Project Editor: Eleanor Castellano
Production Supervisor: Ed Triebe

LINDENMEIER: A PLEISTOCENE
HUNTING SOCIETY

Library of Congress Cataloging in Publication Data

Wilmsen, Edwin N
    Lindenmeier: a Pleistocene hunting society.
    (Harper's case studies in archaeology)
    1. Lindenmeier site, Colo.   I. Title.
E78.C6W54   917.88   73-13205
ISBN 0-06-047153-0

CONTENTS

EDITOR'S FOREWORD

As student interest in anthropology and archaeology has increased in recent years, I have seen a need for a series of supplementary texts such as "Harper's Case Studies in Archaeology." The rapid growth of enrollments in introductory courses and the offering of such courses in ever larger numbers of colleges and universities across the country have placed a considerable strain on the relatively meager resources available, particularly those used in the teaching of archaeology. My concern over the lack of teaching resources in archaeology is shared by many in the profession. I am grateful not only for the positive response to the idea of a series of short monographs reporting problem-oriented archaeological research but also for the commitment of scholars to produce exciting accounts of their current research.

The books in this series are designed to show the methods by which archaeologists solve research problems of broad anthropological significance. The range of problems, time period, and areas of the world studied has been selected to provide maximum utility and flexibility for the teachers of introductory anthropology and archaeology courses. The series will provide an integrated set of monographs that introduce the student to basic aspects of modern archaeological research. There is probably no more effective means to convey the excitement and relevance of modern, problem-oriented archaeological investigation than to have the investigators who conceive and carry out such research prepare the monographs themselves. By providing an integrated view of the most recent directions in archaeological research, the monographs will challenge the instructor to put recent investigations into historical perspective and encourage the student to develop an appreciation of the importance of the development of anthropological archaeology in light of the present thrust of our discipline. The student will also share in the current emphasis upon relevant research designed to reveal the nature of cultural evolution. The emphasis of the series is explicitly upon process—processes of change and stability in the development of culture. As such, the series is designed to contribute to the teaching of modern anthropology and to emphasize the important role that archaeological research plays in achieving the larger goals of anthropology.

THE AUTHOR AND HIS BOOK

Edwin N. Wilmsen is an Associate Professor of Anthropology and a Curator in the Museum of Anthropology at the University of Michigan. He received the Doctor of Philosophy degree in anthropology from the University of Arizona in 1967. Before joining the faculty at the University of Michigan in 1968, Professor Wilmsen taught at the University of Maryland and he was a Research Associate in the Office of Anthropology at the U.S. National Museum, Smithsonian Institution in Washington, D.C.

Like many anthropologists, Professor Wilmsen came into the field after training and professional experience in another discipline. He received a professional degree in architecture in 1959 from the Massachusetts Institute of Technology. He then taught architecture at the University of Texas and joined the faculty in architecture at the University of Arizona as an Assistant Professor in 1960. His growing interest in anthropology led him to begin a doctoral program in 1964, during which time he became concerned with smaller hunting and gathering societies such as those that existed during the Pleistocene. These interests have continued and formed the focus of his current research and the topic of this book.

His interest in small hunting and gathering societies of a type anthropologists call band societies led him to develop powerful new techniques for the analysis of the archaeological remains of such groups. New means for analyzing stone tools were pioneered by Professor Wilmsen and are discussed in some detail in this book. The interested student should read an article that Professor Wilmsen published in *Science*, "Lithic Analysis in Paleoanthropology" (1968), and his important monograph, *Lithic Analysis and Cultural Inference: a Paleo-Indian Case*, published by the University of Arizona Press (1970).

The present book examines one such band society that existed in what is now northern Colorado about 11,000 years ago. The archaeological remains of this hunting and gathering society occur at one of the largest Paleo-Indian sites known in North America, the Lindenmeier Site. It was extensively excavated over several seasons nearly 40 years ago by Frank H. H. Roberts, Jr. of the Smithsonian Institution.

The careful work by Roberts and his excellent recording in the field enabled Professor Wilmsen to undertake an analysis of the archaeological remains many years after they were excavated. The author discusses the work by Roberts in detail, indicating how his own interests differ and how the approach to the study of these remains has changed as the problems themselves have changed.

Wilmsen adopts an ecological approach that focuses his attention on the social organization of the groups that camped at Lindenmeier, their hunting strategies, and the nature of their interaction with other groups of hunters in the area. How the archaeologist gets from stone tools and other archaeological remains to aspects of the organization and behavior of long-extinct societies is one of the important messages for the student in this book.

William A. Longacre

PREFACE

There are many ways to look at the natural world. One such
way is E. B. Cassedy's fantastic global view of the Lindenmeier
region. In it, phenomenological qualities of the landscape are
selectively stressed to form a highly personal statement about
place and time. Notions of space, of form, and of boundaries

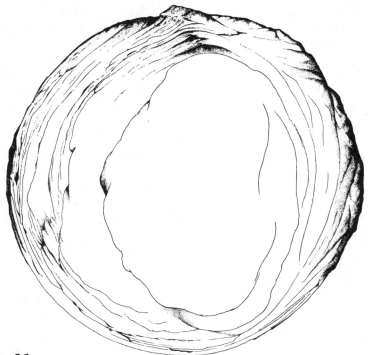

Fig. 0.1

*Satellite view of the Lindenmeier region drawn in 1938. The prom-
inent hill seen to the left center in Fig. 3.3 is at the top of this
drawing. (After a drawing by E. B. Cassedy.)*

have been filtered through the artist's eye. I am sure that Cassedy intended more than the creation of a draftman's *tour de force* and that he wished to express a symbolic worldview that might have been held by the people who made temporary homes in the Lindenmeier Valley. Such an expression can be thought of as a form of truth, for men are irrevocably attached and attracted to some place, and the intepretation of this attachment is open to an infinite number of subjective permutations.

Another view is obtained through the historical record. Historiography (the writing of history) is "true" to the extent that it accurately describes events that took place in the past. Archaeologists have long been engaged in the task of writing a special kind of history—one for which no written record exists. Tools for this task are highly developed: excavating techniques, dating methods, procedures for comparing artifacts and sites. Undoubtedly, the most securely established archaeological work to date is that which has broadened our description of prehistoric events.

Science presents yet another view. Its aims are not solely to interpret or describe but ultimately to explain events in terms that pertain to more than just the events themselves. As these goals are more demanding than are those of other orientations, science can never claim to have attained truth. Thus, scientists must be satisfied with a goal of formulating tentative explanations, called hypotheses, for their observations of the world. Since hypotheses are numerous, varied, and of unequal credibility, it is necessary to submit them to repeated and varied forms of testing. In recent years, some archaeologists have begun the process of strengthening the scientific foundation of their field. It is not an easy task; the direction in which to proceed is not always immediately clear. This book is intended to contribute to the process by introducing students to some of the issues that are basic to these changing archaeological goals.

I hope that, in writing this book, I have made it clear that I do not claim to have attained ultimate answers to centuries old questions. Nor do I suppose that my results are uniformly "better" than are those of my predecessors; in fact, I do not believe that value judgments in science have any relevance except within the context of a particular investigational framework. I have tried to emphasize this relativity of goal to strategy, of result to intention, in my brief consideration of the history of thought about American Indians and in my more detailed analysis of previous work at the Lindenmeier site. Most of my conclusions are, at this moment, as tentative as are those that have been made in the past; as far as dating and stratigraphy are concerned, the results achieved by other workers are on more firmly established ground.

I do wish to emphasize two things, however. First, the date and place of an object—even its comparative association with other objects—are parts of the description of that object. Placement in time or space does not differ in principle from descriptions of the color or shape of the object. Until recently, almost all analytical work in Pleistocene archaeology has been focused on such descriptive measures. Conclusions have been interpretations based upon an individual's intuition and personal experience. The second point I wish to emphasize is that, except in a subjective sense such as that applied to Cassedy's drawings, individual interpretations, taken alone, cannot be shown to conform more or less closely to reality, although some may, in fact, be closer than others. My intention has been to acquaint students with a procedure by which to demonstrate that some conclusions are less tentative than others and to draw new conclusions from established principles rather than from individual experience.

The issues are primarily theoretical and methodological; I have stressed theory and method for this reason. But I have tried to make the presentation as unpretentious as possible and have used currently familiar objects as illustrations whenever it seemed appropriate to do so. Data from the Lindenmeier site in northern Colorado are used throughout the book to give archaeological substance to the arguments that are developed.

The emphasis of my research has been upon the structures of sites and upon the relations of these structures to those of social groups. Such an emphasis poses questions about the organization of groups in space. Can we estimate the sizes of groups? Can we discover the activities which they performed? Can we identify individual groups and their site locations? Can we deduce anything about communication between groups?

Answers to these and other questions require the most detailed analyses of artifact distributions as well as of the artifacts themselves. Perhaps the details of these analyses, especially of the statistical manipulations, will be obscure to some beginning students. But my statistical results are summarized rather than presented in detail as part of a sequence of analytical data reductions. My principal concern is that you understand my particular methods of analysis, not that you follow the computations. Those of you with more statistical training will find enough material to check my conclusions and to work out answers to questions of your own. Students who intend to become professional archaeologists should learn fundamental statistics as soon as possible so that they will feel comfortable with quantitative manipulations of data such as those presented here.

A book such as this one is but a step in a lifetime of intellectual development; it is therefore an outgrowth of a series of relations that have molded its author's outlook upon the world. My late friend, Edward P. Dozier, shared with me his perceptive wisdom and taught me the essence of being an anthropologist. Carl Wilmsen and Lisa Wilmsen continually reintroduced to me the freshness of life as they worked with me on their free weekends. A number of students have participated in the excitement of discovery—and the drudgery of routine work —which was a constant part of the Lindenmeier project: Jerry Voss, John Shea, Herbert Rutledge, Ivor Gross, and Gretchen Baugh. Karen Harbeck, especially, was an invaluable counselor and critic. Polly Wiessner did much of the statistical work, made crucial suggestions, and allowed me to use parts of her as yet unpublished papers. The continuing friendship of all has been one of the greater rewards of the whole endeavor. Finally, readers of this book owe a debt to my 1972 *Introduction to Archaeology* class, the members of which read parts of the rough manuscript and made many clarifying and simplifying suggestions.

Edwin N. Wilmsen

LINDENMEIER:
A PLEISTOCENE
HUNTING
SOCIETY

1. Ideas About the Past

When Renaissance adventurers from Spain, France, and England fought and fumbled their way into North America, it rapidly became clear to them that Columbus had discovered not the Indies but a New World. Everywhere, European explorers were met by peoples previously unheard of whose very existence required explanation. Native Americans were encountered living in conditions ranging from elaborate urban wealth to basic hunting simplicity.

The intellectual history of attempts to account for these people has been marked by dramatic fluctuations of opinion, but from the beginning three questions have been dominant: Where did American Indians come from, when did they arrive, what did they bring with them. It is not surprising, therefore, that questions of origin, chronology, and typology were embraced wholeheartedly in the nineteenth century by those who began to investigate America's archaeological past. These questions have remained paramount among prehistorians, especially those whose interest focuses on the earlier portions of the archaeological record.

ARISTOTLE, THE DEVIL, AND OTHERS

Speculation about Indian ancestors began early. First thoughts turned naturally for guidance to scriptural history and classical literature. Indians, not being mentioned in the Bible, were relegated by many to subhuman status. Others solved the apparent biblical oversight by linking the Indians with the Ten Lost Tribes of Israel who, thus, were thought to have ended their wanderings in America.

Even though most efforts to explain Indian existence sought to build appropriate frameworks of space and time upon which to hang Indian history, the discovery of these peoples contributed to the reexamination of fundamental philosophical questions that was engaging the intellectual interest of Europe.

1

Fig. 1.1

An early nineteenth century European view of peoples native to other continents; all were lumped together into a single uncivilized class. Engraving from The uncivilized races of men in all countries of the world: being a comprehensive account of their manners and customs, and their physical, social, mental, moral and religious characteristics *by J. G. Wood. Published in 1880 by J. B. Burr Publishing Co., Hartford.*

Extensive public debates between scholars raged over the basic issues of human status, of criteria for admitting individuals and populations to that status, and of the rights that accompany it. The most famous of these debates took place in 1550–1551 in Valladolid, Spain, between Bartolomé de Las Casas, who had been Bishop of Chiapas, and Juan Ginés de Sepúlveda, the

Spanish humanist who clung to the doctrine of natural slavery. Las Casas' arguments were influential in the decision of Pope Paul III to issue the bull *Sublimas Deus* in which Indian humanity was decreed and their full human rights declared.

Sublimas Deus did not at once convert everyone to the new dogma, but it did help open the way to more specific attempts to connect the Indians to known and semiknown peoples. Many such groups were invoked by sixteenth-century writers. In 1590, shunning ideas about direct sea or sunken land routes, Fray Jose de Acosta postulated a land bridge in northern latitudes over which small bands of hunters made their way little by little from Asia into America.

Acosta's writings had little impact. Throughout the seventeenth century learned arguments continued between supporters of different Indian ancestors—Ethiopians, Chinese, Scythians, Norsemen, and countless others (Fig. 1.1). It was suggested that Indians were refugees from Plato's sunken Atlantis. A few scholars found the question so difficult that it continued to be easier for them to invoke Aristotle's concept of spontaneous generation, developed to account for "secondary" animals such as frogs and flies, than to attempt connections with distant and isolated peoples.

Among later speculators were several historically prominant Americans. Cotton Mather in 1702 believed that "the devil had decoyed these miserable savages" to America so that he could hold "absolute empire over them." Thomas Jefferson thought that the great diversity of American languages was evidence of an American homeland for Asian peoples. Benjamin Franklin and Noah Webster took such a limited view of prehistory that they attributed the great earthworks of the South and Midwest to DeSoto, the sixteenth-century Spanish explorer, and his men. Toward the end of the nineteenth century, Louis Agassiz still maintained that native populations had an independent history of origin in the New World.

THE IDEA OF PREHISTORY AND THE PALEOLITHIC

Major scientific events, which in nineteenth-century Europe followed each other in rapid succession, undermined scriptural dogma and played an important role in shaping American thoughts about the prehistory of this continent. The demonstration of stratigraphic succession in geologic processes made by Hutton, Lyell, and Smith; Agassiz's delineation of Pleistocene glacial events; and the concept of evolution synthesized by Darwin and Wallace, forever changed contemporary views of the world. It was probably no accident that in both England and France in the same year, 1859, associations of human implements with long extinct animals were first generally accepted.

Sir John Lubbock published his book *Prehistoric Times* in 1868. It was the first synthesis of then current ideas about an epoch of human evolution before recorded history. Sir John introduced the concept of a paleolithic stage (Greek: *palaios* = old + *lithos* = stone) which he associated with a geologically remote time during which anatomically primitive men hunted no-longer living forms of animals with crude stone tools. Many discoveries of handaxes and flakes in river gravels and caves came to light and were assigned to this stage.

Paleolithic men were suddenly well established in European thought and this was bound to be followed quickly in America. There was not much enthusiasm for early prehistory on this continent until European sites of assumed great age became known; these discoveries then became the standard against which American evidence was measured. The question of origins became secondary and antiquity was sought. During the second half of the century, the presumed age of the earliest American settlement was pushed farther and farther back in time.

But evidence for such great antiquity was at best flimsy. By 1890, a strong reaction set in and the then-supposed recency of man's first entry into the New World reduced scholarly interest in the question. Bitter recriminations were leveled at those who suggested "respectable" antiquity for their finds. W. H. Holmes of the U.S. National Museum "felt it a duty to hold and enforce the view" that evidence for relatively early men in America was "not only inadequate but dangerous to the cause of science." This was in 1925.

The discovery, a year later, of artifacts in clear association with skeletons of extinct bison reopened the discussion and initiated a period of vigorous fieldwork. The Folsom site in northeastern New Mexico, at which this discovery was made, has given its name to a distinctive category of implements (stone projectile points), to a phase in the prehistory of this continent, and even to a "people" with its attendant "culture." A number of important sites were identified during the next decade. Some, including Lindenmeier, had been known to amateur collectors for many years, but their relation to an early period had not been suspected. The questions of origin and antiquity were raised again, this time within the frame of reference provided by glacial geologists.

Inflated speculations of great age continued—and continue

—to be made, but a greater understanding of geohistory and culture history have made such claims increasingly untenable. The important problems of the future will not be concerned with origins and age as major issues in themselves. Rather, they will be focused upon the principles of organization that characterize hunting societies.

PREVIEW TO A DIFFERENT APPROACH

The organizational structure of a society consists of the set of recurrent ways in which individuals arrange themselves with respect to each other at different times in order to cope with some social or ecological condition. The roles of producer, parent, associate, and kinsman are combined into a structure within which a society's members go about their business. Population movements, group formation and maintenance, and resource procurement strategies are all parts of a society's organizational structure. Place and time are simply scales of measurement; they are important descriptors but they can do no more than add to a catalogue of information about a site or series of sites. Organizational studies are at least potentially deducible from general principles. They subsume time and place, and if well designed, can give an account of relations between parts of a social system. They are consequently more capable of providing answers to questions about the operation of societies than are other kinds of studies.

Focus on such details as the angles of tool edges is a means by which to answer limited questions about organizational structure. Edge angles, for instance, are necessary components in a study of ecological variation and functional application of tools. They can help clarify our understanding of the ways in which individuals keep themselves supplied with the necessities of life, and, thus, can be useful in discovering the relationships between groups and environmental elements.

This book will be concerned with such organizational problems, but a quick overview of my understanding of what is now known about origins and age will be needed to set the stage for more detailed discussion and will give those students who wish to dig deeper into Paleo-Indian literature a clear impression of the bias which underlies this study.

Geographic expansion is one of the outstanding characteristics of the Upper Paleolithic period; it took people into all of northern Asia and the Western Hemisphere for the first time and approximately doubled the land area occupied by them.

In understanding Indian origins, however, we have hardly

passed beyond Acosta's postulate made 400 years ago: a land bridge in northern latitudes over which small bands of hunters made their way little by little from Asia into America. We are reasonably sure of Asia; there is no defensible alternative. The existence of a land bridge across the Bering Strait, as wide as the north-south dimension of Alaska, connecting Siberia and Alaska at intervals throughout the Pleistocene has been well documented. The last of these connections was exposed from 12,000 to 20,000 years ago; most archaeologists estimate that the first human inhabitants of North America came into the continent during this time. But the processes by which "small bands made their way little by little" are still obscure.

Nonetheless, a number of things seem more likely than others. The movement of peoples across northern Asia into North America probably accompanied a whole series of developments in the ways in which people formed groups, in the methods employed to obtain plant and animal food, and in the mechanisms for maintaining contacts between groups. Along with these developments, techniques for coping with Arctic and Boreal environments must have come into being—for example, techniques for sewing clothing, building shelters that could provide protection from cold, and for cutting frozen meat. Some of these innovations may have been made thousands of years before people moved into Siberia; some probably came into existence during the preceding Middle Paleolithic period. How these innovations originated is not yet known, but they first appear clearly together as a coherent system in the Upper Paleolithic of Eurasia beginning about 40,000 years ago.

An understanding of how the continent was populated is thus most productively sought in an understanding of strategies for obtaining food, of group organizations for activating these strategies, and of the processes of tool manufacture and use that characterized paleolithic Eurasia during the later phases of pleistocene glaciation. This statement implies that there can be no specific origin, in the usual historical sense, for native American populations but that their derivation must be considered to be a function of spatial diffusion processes which brought about an extraordinary expansion of human populations during the final phases of the Paleolithic.

These processes operated throughout the frontier between populated and unpopulated spaces. Local conditions along some part of the frontier may have temporarily favored more rapid colonization, but over a period of time such conditions probably fluctuated widely along the entire frontier and no single region was favored consistantly over others. Although colonization

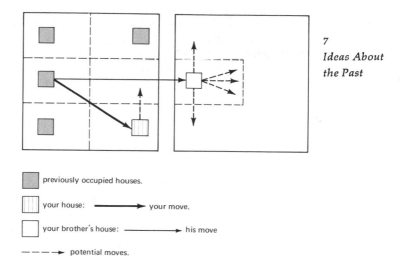

previously occupied houses.

your house: ⟶ your move.

your brother's house: ⟶ his move

— — — ⟶ potential moves.

Fig. 1.2

*Colonization of empty lots and blocks. Black squares
represent previously occupied houses. Gray square is
your house; heavy arrow is your move. Your brother's house is the white square; the light arrow is his
move. Dashed arrows represent potential moves.*

proceeded irregularly, we must assume that social ties between
groups (for economic assistance and mate selection, for examples) remained necessary and that, once formed, it was advantageous to maintain those ties already in existence rather
than to establish new ones. Colonizing groups would benefit
by moving to places where associations with friends and kinsmen could be retained instead of moving to more isolated locations. If existing networks between groups were not retained,
pioneering units would be isolated from any form of social
cooperation—assistance in hunting, access to marriage partners
and the services of curers, participation in ritual observances—
and would not long have survived. There is a sound, practical
advantage in keeping lines of social interaction open; had they
not been open during the late Pleistocene, America may not
have been settled until Columbus arrived.

A subjective example will illustrate the process: Imagine a
city block on which all the houses are occupied by the families
of your relatives (including your parents) and close friends but
which contains some vacant lots; at an appropriate time you
marry and build a house for your new family on one of the

vacant lots. Strictly speaking, you will have left your former home. But your social contacts will not have been severed, and your network of social interaction, although probably altered by your new status, will remain intact; your new territory (your lot) will no doubt have long been familiar to you. You would hardly say that you had moved "away." Imagine further that your brother, again at an appropriate time, builds across the street—or, perhaps, a short distance down the road—on a previously unoccupied block and, thus, opens a new area to settlement. The same statements about the retention of social ties made about your move apply to him. Again, you would not say that he had moved away, but he has begun the settlement of a new area (Fig. 1.2).

I would argue that our Pleistocene case is analogous to that just illustrated, assuming that individual and group movements were made with minimum disruption of established social networks, and that new territory was entered as necessary and as eligible individuals reached appropriate status to move. Group emigration, accordingly, must have been rare, and most groups were probably geographically stable. Clearly, the problem of origins is an organizational one and thus a special case of the problems investigated in this book. Although I will not be concerned with origins directly, certain facets of the colonization process will be clarified during the course of the analysis presented in the following chapters.

REFERENCES

Daniel, Glynn
    1963   *The Idea of Prehistory.* Cleveland and New York, World.
Hanke, Lewis
    1949   *The Spanish Struggle for Justice in the Conquest of America.* Philadelphia, University of Pennsylvania Press.
Haven, Samuel F.
    1856   Archaeology in the United States. *Smithsonian Contributions to Knowledge,* Vol. 8, pp. 1–168.
Hopkins, David M.
    1959   Cenozoic history of the Bering land bridge. *Science,* Vol. 129, pp. 1519–1528.
Joint Symposium of the American Anthropological Association and the American Association for the Advancement of Science, Section H.
    1912   The problems of the unity or plurality and the probable place of origin of the American aboriginies. *American Anthropologist,* Vol. 14, pp. 1–59.

MacNeish, Richard S. (ed.)
  1973 *Early Man in America: Readings from Scientific American.*
        San Francisco, Freeman.
Wauchope, Robert
  1962 *Lost Tribes and Sunken Continents.* Chicago, University of
        Chicago Press.
Wilmsen, Edwin N.
  1965 An outline of early man studies in the United States. *American Antiquity,* Vol. 31, pp. 172–192.

2. Background in Time and Place

In 1940, Frank Roberts introduced the name "Paleo-Indian" in the title of his cumulative synthesis of work in Americanist early man studies. He did not define the term and, in fact, used it only once in his text. But it is clear that he was referring to hunting peoples represented by sites associated with extinct animals and presumed to date to the final portions of the Pleistocene. This label was immediately adopted and has remained in use with essentially unchanged meaning.

The landscape in which these paleolithic populations lived was much as it is today except that vegetation zones were displaced southward during glacial advances; they returned northward as glaciers retreated. Tundra and open boreal forest were dominant farther south than now during those times when ice covered much of the northern portion of the hemisphere. Just as today habitats vary according to latitude and local topography, so in the past a variety of life zones prevailed according to local conditions.

In Eurasia, reindeer (caribou), bison, horse, mammoth, and other large species were hunted. Horses were absent in America, but giant bison and mammoth were extensively hunted until about 10,000 years ago when these species, too, became extinct and the faunal assemblage of the continent became established in its modern form. Everywhere, during the Pleistocene and after, many other mammalian species, large and small, were important parts of man's food supply.

Although we have little substantiating evidence, a variety of plant foods was probably used in season. Evidence is accumulating that fish and sea mammals were eaten in some, if not all, parts of the world during the Upper Paleolithic. Fluctuation in seasonal and long-term cycles of productivity in both plant and animal communities must have been as great then as now. The survival of a hunting group depends upon its ability to predict food conditions in different parts of its territory and to take advantage of these predictions. That these late paleolithic hunt-

ing and gathering peoples were successful is demonstrated by
the fact that their descendants populated two previously unoccupied American continents in addition to vast areas of the
Old World.

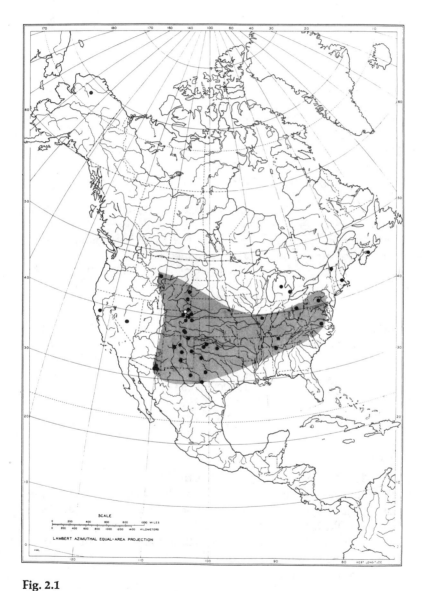

Fig. 2.1

*Location of known fluted point sites. Each dot marks the location of
one site; Lindenmeier is marked by a star. Fluted points are found in
greatest number within the shaded area.*

Table 2.1

*Ages of Fluted Point Sites; Only Sites with Radiocarbon Age
Determinations Are Included.*

Site	Age	s	Age − 2s	Age + 2s
Lubbock	9883 ±	350	9183 yrs.	10583 yrs.
Bonfire Shelter	10230 ±	160		
Blackwater (Folsom level)	10250 ±	320		
Debert	10600 ±	47		
Hell Gap	10850 ±	550		
Lindenmeier	10780 ±	375		
	11200 ±	400		
Lehner	11170 ±	140		
Dent	11200 ±	500		
Domebo	11220 ±	500		
Murray Springs	11230 ±	340		
Blackwater (Clovis level)	11260 ±	420	10420 yrs.	12100 yrs.

Minimum   probable = least age for oldest site minus greatest
difference between age   age for youngest site
span   = (Blackwater Age − 2s) − (Lubbock   Age
                          + 2s)
                     = 10420 − 10583
                     = − 163 yrs.

Maximum   probable = greatest age for oldest site minus least
difference between age   age for youngest site
span   = (Blackwater Age + 2s) − (Lubbock   Age
                          − 2s)
                     = 12100 − 9183
                     = 2917 yrs.

By 11,000 years ago, all of North America that was free of
ice cover was occupied by peoples with a basic Eurasian Upper
Paleolithic way of life. We call these hunting peoples Paleo-
Indians (Old or Ancient Indians). Lindenmeier was one of their
campsites; we will turn our attention first to its place in the
standard archaeological record and then to its history before
considering its contents.

The map (Fig. 2.1) shows the location of all the major sites
with fluted points that have so far been recorded. In addition,
isolated fluted points are continually found eroding from the
present ground surface and out of stream banks. Thousands of

specimens have been found in such nonassociated contexts; nearly 500 with reasonably exact information on find location have been reported from Ohio alone and over 100 are reported from around St. Louis. Similarly large numbers are reported from many other states. It is probably no exaggerated guess to estimate that 10,000 fluted points are in the collections of amateurs. Clearly, these implements are widely distributed over the continent. The shaded area of the map indicates the densest concentration of fluted point discoveries. A few such points have been found in western Canada, Alaska, Mexico, and Central America. At least one site, El Inga in Peru, is known in South America.

The time at which these sites were occupied can be reasonably estimated through the use of the radiocarbon dating technique. All of the currently available radiocarbon ages of sites containing fluted points are given in Table 2.1.

The radiocarbon technique is one of statistical chemistry in which the proportion of the unstable radioactive isotope of carbon, ^{14}C, to the stable "dead" isotope, ^{12}C, is measured. Through respiration all living organisms exchange carbon with the atmosphere and incorporate some of this element into their tissues. When an organism dies, it continues to lose ^{14}C because of the instability of this isotope, but no new carbon is taken in to replace it. The rate of radioactive decay of ^{14}C is known and thus it is possible to estimate the amount of elapsed time since an organism's death. The rate is also known to fluctuate, but a consideration of this problem is beyond the intended scope of this book. Wood charcoal is the best material to analyze, but reasonable results may sometimes be obtained from other materials. There is an inherent probability of laboratory counting error in the method which is expressed as the standard deviation of the given age and is written as a plus-or-minus ($\pm$) value after the determined age. There is a 68 percent chance that the measured age of an analyzed *specimen* falls within one standard deviation of the determined value and a 95 percent chance that it falls within two standard deviations. The true age of a *site* depends, in addition, upon at least two other factors: the analyzed specimen must have been deposited at the same time as the rest of the cultural material that it is intended to date, and the specimen must be free of contamination. Thus, radiocarbon analysis provides an *estimate* of age, not an *absolute* date.

This brief outline of the radiocarbon method is highly simplified, but it is detailed enough to allow one to follow the reasoning that underlies the computation given in Table 2.1. The

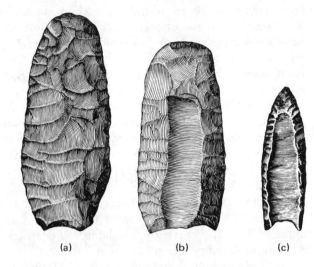

(a)   (b)   (c)

Fig. 2.2

Stages in the production of a fluted point: (a) bi-facially flaked preform which has been chipped into shape; (b) preform which has been given a more regular form and from which one flute has been re-moved; (c) finished Folsom point, the flute is shaded. After drawings by E. B. Cassedy. (By permission of the Smithsonian Institution.)

period of time that fluted points were made was almost cer-tainly quite short. For those sites that have been dated, the maximum difference in age is less than 3000 years. We may infer that the other known sites and those yet to be discovered will fall within the same time span.

Fluted points of different types, because of their distinctive forms, have come to be regarded as the diagnostic indicators of Paleo-Indian sites. In order to understand parts of this book, you will need to know something about fluted points and the process of fluting. Figure 2.2 depicts a series of specimens in different stages of fluting. The procedure has been well de-scribed by Don Crabtree, who has spent 40 years experimenting with flaking processes. The following steps seem to have been taken:

1. A suitable flake was selected and chipped on both surfaces to give it a regular shape.

2. The blank was given a lanceolate form and was reduced in thickness; the tip end was left thick to absorb the fluting blow.

3. Flutes were struck from both faces, probably with the aid of an intermediate punch, while the tip was supported on a solid anvil.

4. The edges were finished, and the point was given its final form.

Several types of fluted points have been defined and named. Excellent descriptions and type definitions of all Paleo-Indian point forms appear in Marie Wormington's book Ancient man in North America.

In summary, Paleo-Indians lived in North America at the very end of the Pleistocene in an environment slightly cooler perhaps than today's and in a landscape that was somewhat more varied but not unlike that of today. Their entire livelihood was gained by hunting and gathering wild resources. They made and used a kind of spear point that was one of the finest products of flintnapping technology ever created. Lindenmeier, which we will now consider in detail, is one of the largest Paleo-Indian sites ever discovered.

REFERENCES

Crabtree, Don E.
   1966 A stoneworker's approach to analyzing and replicating the Lindenmeier Folsom. *Tebiwa, The Journal of the Idaho State University Museum*, Vol. 9, No. 1.
Fitting, James, Jerry De Visscher, and Edward J. Wahla
   1966 The Paleo-Indian occupation of Holcombe Beach. *University of Michigan Museum of Anthropology, Anthropological Papers*, No. 27.
Haury, Emil W., E. B. Sayles, and W. W. Wasley
   1959 The Lehner mammoth site, southwestern Arizona. *American Antiquity*, Vol. 25, pp. 2–30.
Haynes, C. Vance
   1964 Fluted projectile points: their age and dispersion. *Science*, Vol. 145, pp. 1408–1413.
MacDonald, George
   1968 Debert: a Paleo-Indian campsite in central Nova Scotia. *National Museum of Canada, Anthropology Papers*, No. 16.

Mason, Roland J.
    1962   The Paleo-Indian tradition in eastern North America. *Current Anthropology*, Vol. 3, pp. 227–278.
Roberts, Frank H. H., Jr.
    1940   Developments in the problem of the North American Paleo-Indian. *Smithsonian Miscellaneous Collections*, Vol. 100:51–116.
Warnica, James M.
    1966   New discoveries at the Clovis site. *American Antiquity*, Vol. 31, pp. 345–357.
Wormington, H. Marie
    1957   Ancient man in North America. *Denver Museum of Natural History, Popular Series*, No. 4.

3. Lindenmeier

The Lindenmeier site is located in Larimer County, Colorado, about 46 kilometers north of the city of Ft. Collins and 2.8 kilometers south of the Wyoming state line.

NATURAL SETTING

The site lies at an elevation of 2006 meters, almost precisely on the point of intersection of three major physiographic subdivisions: the Rocky Mountain Front Range, the Colorado Piedmont, and the High Plains. It is situated on a small, benchlike valley remnant on the side of the first foothill ridge of the Rockies. The foothills have formed fingerlike extensions that here project farther eastward onto the Plains than at any other place.

The piedmont, a huge, shallow basin eroded below the surface of the High Plains by the South Platte River and its tributaries, abuts these ridges. As a result, when standing on the site one sees a seemingly endless, gently undulating plain extending to the east and south (Fig. 3.1). Within 150 meters to the north, a ridge some 60 meters high contains the valley bottom before dropping off again to the next valley floor. Westward, the foothills proper rise in a series of tilted uplifts to the crest of the Rockies and culminate in Long's Peak at an elevation of 4345 meters (Fig. 3.2).

The Lindenmeier Valley is almost completely flat over much of its area but slopes gently upward to the base of "Folsom Man Hill" on its western edge (Fig. 3.3). It is only a quarter of a mile wide and about two miles long, and its topography was not very different at the time of its initial human occupation. The basal formation is a white Oligocene clay (called Brule by geologists), which is impervious to surface water perculation but which will transmit ground water by capillary action. This factor was probably important in the occupation of the valley and the surrounding area because springs and groundwater

Fig. 3.1

View from Lindenmeier toward southeast. The Plains and Colorado Piedmont stretch to the horizon and beyond. Photo taken by F. H. H. Roberts, Jr.

soaks, which are still prominent features of the foothill-piedmont margin, emerge at the Brule contact surface, and large wet-meadows are formed (Fig. 3.4).

The strata which overlie the Brule at Lindenmeier are most economically interpreted as wet-meadow deposits. In sharp contrast to the white clay, these strata, rich in organic matter, are dark grey to black and are easily distinguished visually from the underlying Brule formation. These layered deposits are the products of anaerobic (living in the absence of free oxygen) decay processes which take place in thick, wet vegetation and are characteristic of locations which have standing water for at least part of every year. Analyses of soil samples taken from the site have yielded results expected for soils of this kind. Mollusks present in the soil and collected during the course of excavation include species (*Vertigo* sp., *Succinea grovenori*) that require slow-moving—but not stagnant—water as part of their habitat.

Shallow ponds associated with a small, possibly intermittent, springfed, meandering stream or a series of seeps were to be found in the valley floor during late Pleistocene time. Water collected in slight depressions in the ground surface and was retained by the underlying clay. As plant decay products and slope-washed soil accumulated in a depression, its bottom was raised, water was diverted to lower areas, and the cycle was repeated.

Sediments contained in a bison bone taken from the site have been analyzed for pollen (Table 3.1). From the result, we may infer the vegetation which grew in the valley at the time of the Folsom occupation: grasses, sedges, and composites (sunflowers, asters, daisies, and other familiar flowering plants of the Plains and mountains) probably formed a fairly lush groundcover. Although pine pollen is heavily represented in the spectrum, pine trees did not necessarily grow in the valley itself. Pine pollen is easily transported on the wind for great distances and is dominant in samples taken from the present surface even though the nearest stand of pines is several miles away. The presence of spruce pollen, however—even in the small amount indicated—probably means that spruce grew in the valley or on its adjacent slopes, as its pollen is not often transported very far from its source.

Fig. 3.2

View across Lindenmeier to the south; Long's Peak is in the background. The site lies between the arroyo and the valley edge. Photo taken by F. H. H. Roberts, Jr.

Fig. 3.3

Upper end of the Lindenmeier valley to west of the site showing how the mountains immediately begin to rise. Photo taken by F. H. H. Roberts, Jr.

We may, then, picture the Lindenmeier Valley as a small, well-watered platform which supported a rich meadow vegetation with some coniferous trees and perhaps a few oaks. Similar valleys are found at slightly higher elevations today. Like them, the Lindenmeier Valley of 11,000 years ago was only a few miles from heavily wooded, stream-dissected mountains; it was even closer to the relatively dry High Plains grasslands.

The associated fauna is characteristic of these several habitat varieties. The fossil bison which form such a conspicuous part of the faunal assemblage have attracted the most attention. However, the remains of other animals should not be overlooked, because they too are important to an understanding of the human occupation of this valley. Table 3.2 lists all the species recovered.

The bison species, *Bison antiquus* Leidy, differs from the modern species, *Bison bison*, in several important ways. These differences are of the kind expected if these species lived in different habitats—*antiquus* in open meadow parkland and *bison* on dry steppe plains. *Antiquus* was larger than *bison* in body proportions by about 20 percent but its head and horns were more than twice as large. This kind of animal would have been at home in the Lindenmeier Valley and throughout the mountain-basin province.

None of the other animals were different from their modern descendents. With the exception of pronghorn and jackrabbits (which prefer dryer habitat zones), they would have found the valley well suited to their needs. These species live in amazingly large numbers on the nearby plains and would have been equally available 11,000 years ago. Foxes and coyotes are still abundant in the area; wolves, of course, have been exterminated within the last century.

The faunal assemblage, thus, is principally one characteristic of a well-watered, grassy environment with scattered stands of trees and bushy cover. Bison were at least part-time residents in the valley. Pronghorn and jackrabbits were probably brought to the site from other habitat zones that were not more than 10 kilometers away. Foxes, coyotes, and wolves would have ranged over all these zones.

Toward the end of the Pleistocene, conditions which led to

Fig. 3.4

One of several wet meadows that exist near Lindenmeier today. If a few trees were added to the picture, a good impression of the probable appearance of the Pleistocene Lindenmeier Valley would be given. Photo taken by F. H. H. Roberts, Jr.

Table 3.1

Pollen Present in Sediments Taken from a Bison Horn Core.
(Analysis by Vorsila Bohrer.)

POLLEN TYPE		PROPORTION TO TOTAL ($N = 200$)
Pinus	pine	.820
Picea	spruce	.020
Quercus	oak	.015
Ephedra		.010
Gramineae	grasses	.030
Cyperaceae	sedges	.005
Chenopodiaceae		.025
Sarcobatos	greasewood	.005
Compositae	sunflowers, etc.	.070
		1.000

Juniperus (juniper) and *Salix* (willow) were detected by examinations of microfossils present in the sediments and of charcoal from fire scatters.

meadow formation came to an end. Headward erosion by a companion stream, now called Sand Creek, truncated the upper end of the Lindenmeier Valley and robbed it of its water sources. Erosional debris from higher ground then covered the valley bottom and preserved the cultural material.

THE EXCAVATIONS: GOALS AND STRATEGIES

The Lindenmeier site was first discovered by Judge Clyde C. Coffin and his son in 1924. The site takes its name from William Lindenmeier, Jr., who owned the horse ranch upon which it was found. Judge Coffin and his brother, Major Roy G. Coffin, were ardent amateur collectors of Indian relics and both had an extensive knowledge of the prehistoric remains commonly found in Colorado and Wyoming. The Coffins were convinced that their Lindenmeier collection represented a type of artifactual assemblage different from that usually found in the area, but not until the Folsom discovery was widely publicized did they recognize its status as an indicator of early human occupation on this continent. Major Coffin must have been a persistent correspondent, for it was only through a series of letters to members of the U.S. Geological Survey and the U.S. National Museum that he awakened professional interest in the site. A geologist himself, Major Coffin maintained a lifelong interest in Lindenmeier and published some brief papers about his work there.

Coffin's letters eventually came to the attention of Frank H. H. Roberts, Jr., an archaeologist in the Bureau of American Ethnography. In 1934, Roberts visited Lindenmeier and began the first of seven seasons' work at the site. His excavation strategy varied from year to year according to his investigational goals. It is instructive to examine these strategies in terms of their associated goals.

The first season's work, in 1934, was undertaken simply to evaluate the site and to estimate its potential for increasing the amount of information about the "presumably early hunting people" represented at Folsom. Roberts established three criteria for judgment: First, the presence of Folsom points, second, the quantity and variety of other included materials, and third, the size of the site. The strategy consisted of two parts. He first walked over an extensive area along the fossil valley in which the site lies in order to estimate the extent of artifact distribution. Such estimates were made possible because the tilt of the modern ground surface is in a different direction from that of the ancient Lindenmeier surface and the two intersect in such a way that artifacts are exposed as the modern surface slowly erodes (Fig. 3.5a). An arroyo also cuts part of the site and exposes more deeply buried parts of the artifact-containing strata. Roberts found artifacts and bones in several places over a distance of a quarter of a mile. Having located areas of artifact and bone concentration, he excavated a small section in the arroyo wall to determine the nature of the preserved material (Fig. 3.6); he wrote, "In view of the small size of the excavation the number of specimens obtained was gratifying both as to quantity and variety" (1935:15).

Table 3.2

Animal Species Represented by Bones in the Lindenmeier Collection.

Antelocapra americana	pronghorn
Bison antiquus	bison (extinct form)
Canis lupus	wolf
Canis latrans	coyote
Vulpes velox	swift fox
Vulpes fulva	red fox
Lepus townsendii	jackrabbit

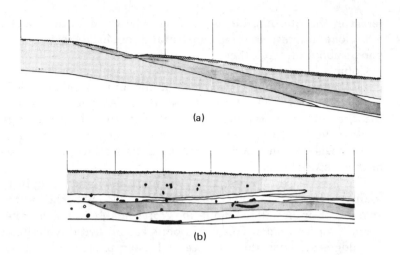

(a)

(b)

Fig. 3.5

Two representative stratigraphic profiles: (a) the ancient surfaces slope more steeply than does the modern surface and are consequently exposed as the latter is lowered by erosion; (b) drawing of a section which is perpendicular to (a). Hearths, heavy black areas, are shown on three different surfaces.

Roberts' conclusions are best given in his own words:

At the Lindenmeier site in northern Colorado is the first occupation level yet found which can be definitely correlated with the makers of the now well-known Folsom points. Distinct traces of a former campsite and workshop are present at this location. Midden deposits have yielded a series of implements actually associated in situ with typical Folsom points. Similar tools have been found at various surface sites, but this is the first evidence to demonstrate that they belonged to the Folsom complex. In addition to the assortment of artifacts, there are flakes, spalls, and nodules, indicating that the implements were made on the spot. Furthermore, this chipper's debris gives good clues to some of the methods used in shaping the tools. The artifacts in the collection show that the lithic component in the local culture pattern was primarily a flake industry, only a few implements of the core type being found. Cut, broken, and split animal bones from the deposits have been identified as being from bison, fox, wolf, and rabbit. The bison remains indicate that those ani-

mals belonged to the same extinct species as those found at
the original Folsom quarry. This is a significant link between
the two sites. (1935:32)

The major goals for the second season's work, 1935, were
geological; Roberts wanted to establish the stratigraphic position of the artifact-bearing sediments and, if possible, to estimate their age. His strategy was direct and simple: two trenches,
each 10 feet wide, were dug beginning on the south side of the
terrace at points where artifacts had been found on the surface
during the previous season's survey. Both of these trenches
were oriented toward the pit dug into the arroyo wall in 1934.
Only one trench was excavated all the way across the terrace
(Fig. 3.7); the second was found to duplicate the information
obtained from the first. Roberts felt that such duplication was
a waste of time and effort; consequently he discontinued work

Fig. 3.6

*The 1934 Big Pit excavations in the arroyo wall. At this point, the
season's work was about half completed. The man is standing on the
level at which artifacts were found. Photo taken by F. H. H. Roberts,
Jr.*

Fig. 3.7

Trench A in the final stages of excavation. Remnants of the Big Pit can be seen on either side. Earth moving equipment, 1930's style, is at work in the background. Photo taken by F. H. H. Roberts, Jr. (By permission of the Smithsonian Institution.)

on the second trench. Again, Roberts' conclusions are most appropriately and succinctly given in his own words:

> Interesting evidence on one of the "burning issues" in the archaeology of the western plains area, the Folsom-Yuma problem, was obtained from the investigations. Stratigraphic material demonstrated that as far as the Lindenmeier site is concerned there was only a very late contemporaneity between Folsom and Yuma points, the Yuma appearing toward the end of the Folsom occupation and surviving longer. Furthermore, Yuma points constitute so small a factor that it is questionable whether they should be considered as belonging to the complex. . . . The large trenches revealed in cross-section the deposits overlying the old level of occupation and demonstrated that what now constitutes a terrace was at one

time an old valley bottom. The ridge that bordered its southern side has been eroded away since the area was abandoned
by its aboriginal occupants. The nature of the valley fill, as
exposed in the trench walls suggests that the changes which
culminated in the present state of the site could not have been
extremely rapid ones. Considerable time must have elapsed
since the layer containing the man-made objects was laid
down. Evidence in the trenches also indicated that the makers
of the tools and the Folsom points stopped for a time along
the slope above the old valley bottom. If the trenches did not
cross a portion of the real campsite, they at least bordered on
it. This was shown by the finding of cut and burned bones,
charcoal and wood ashes, hammerstones and chipper's debris,
and implements broken in the making. All were so situated
that their locations could not be attributed to drift or to the
washing down of material from higher levels. The broken
implements, when the fragments are fitted together and the
original flake is restored, give good evidence of the technique
used in the manufacture of tools.

The trenches did not produce data that are of aid in deter-
mining the age of the site. Despite their establishing the fact
that the soil layer in which the objects are found was pro-
duced by the natural decay and break-up of the top of the
Oligocene bed underlying the area, they gave no clue either
to the agency that originally eroded away the overburden,
thus laying bare the Tertiary stratum and forming the old
valley, or to the time when the action took place. Conditions
at the Clovis lake beds are somewhat better from the stand-
point of dating, and Dr. Ernst Antevs has reached the conclusion, from extensive studies of the area, that the Folsom
artifacts found there represent an antiquity of from 12,000
to 13,000 years. Since the Clovis material indicates that it
comprises the relics of a people whose material culture was
similar to that of the group occupying the Lindenmeier site,
it may be suggested that the latter was approximately the
same age. This should not be regarded as an established fact;
it is merely a postulation based on analogy. Subsequent work
may show the two sites to have been as widely separated in
time as they are in space. There is still an opportunity to
obtain a geologic date for the Lindenmeier site through a
study of the terrace system of the South Platte River and the
relation of its terraces to the glaciation in the Rocky Mountains to the west. The Lindenmeier terrace can be correlated
with those of the South Platte, but as yet there has been no

Fig. 3.8

Excavation in progress in Unit B. A plot of specimens is being made. Photo taken by F. H. H. Roberts, Jr.

determination of the ages of the latter. An attempt to solve this particular problem will constitute a part of the program for future work in the region. (1936:34–36)

There were several secondary goals implicit in the second season's work: to find skeletal remains of "Folsom man," to find evidence of the house types used by these men, and, once more, to increase the quantity and variety of the artifactual assemblage. The latter goal became less important in subsequent years; indeed, in the last three seasons (1938–1940) all chipping debris and many other stone items that were not obviously tools, along with most animal bones, were counted, catalogued —and discarded.

But the search for "Folsom man" and his shelters became the major goal of the remaining explorations.

No human remains have been found, and so far as his physical characteristics are concerned, Folsom man is still a *persona incognita*. There is no evidence as to what type of shelter he may have used . . . it is not likely that his dwelling consisted of anything more substantial than a tent made from the skins of an animal. Traces of the places where he pitched his shelter will be extremely hard to find at this late date. A hard packed floor and hearth, perhaps some post molds, is the most that can be expected. He probably tarried as long at the Lindenmeier camp as he did at any of his settlements, possibly longer than at most of them when its advantages are recalled. Hence the chances of locating a lodge site or even of uncovering his own remains are not altogether beyond the bounds of likelihood. (Roberts 1935:36)

The strategy employed in the field seasons from 1936 through 1940 called for the excavation of large areas with maximum exposure of the levels on which artifacts lay (Figs. 3.8, 3.9). These levels were followed until artifact density became very low; in this way, almost complete living floors were uncovered. Despite these efforts, no human skeletons—or even parts of

Fig. 3.9

Part of the excavation in Unit F. The stakes mark the corners of squares still to be dug. About one-third of the total area uncovered in 1939 is shown; the 1940 excavations continued the expansion of this area. Photo taken by F. H. H. Roberts, Jr.

skeletons—were found. Roberts' disappointment in this negative result is apparent in this statement from his report for the next to last year at Lindenmeier:

> The 1939 season, like its predecessors, failed to produce any human bones, and the physical nature of Folsom man is still unknown. There is no satisfactory explanation for the lack of skeletal materials. It probably is present and simply has not been found in the digging. (1940:92)

The next year, 1940, was the last Roberts worked at Lindenmeier. Other duties—he became Director of the River Basin Survey of the Bureau of American Ethnology—and, undoubtedly, a feeling that there was little left to say about the site delayed the preparation of a final report. The collection remained boxed in storage until Roberts retired in 1964. He intended to spend part of his last years reexamining the collection and making at least a basic description of its contents available to other archaeologists. But his health failed and he was unable to carry out these plans.

CHANGING ISSUES, CHANGING GOALS

It is clear that Roberts' changing goals were contingent upon changes in a more general view of currently important issues in American prehistory: the familiar questions about typology, chronology, and origins. Thus, Roberts' first goal stemmed from a need to confirm the typological association of artifacts and extinct animals recorded at Folsom: His units of analysis were the fluted Folsom point and an extinct form of bison (*Bison antiquus*). The association of these forms was, of course, established.

But the demonstration of an association is not enough, by itself, to place that association in temporal and spatial contexts relative to other known, but different, assemblages. Indeed, some well-known and highly respected anthropologists, A. L. Kroeber and Alĕs Hrdlička among them, were of the opinion that *Bison antiquus* and other no longer living species were not long extinct and, consequently, that Folsom material was not necessarily older than the early agricultural Basketmaker period in the Southwest.

The possibility of a late survival of Pleistocene fauna had been suggested in the early 1920s. William Duncan Strong, an archaeologist, has stated that archaeologists and paleontologists were more willing to grant recency to mammoths and other

extinct animals than anthropologists were to grant antiquity to
American Indians. Hrdlička went so far as to label the Folsom
discoveries neolithic, isolated, and superficial; he said that the
Pleistocene animals associated with these discoveries were "the
Achilles' heel of American archaeology because they were not
long extinct."

Roberts, of course, was aware of this controversy and anxious
to help resolve it. Thus, having settled the typological question
to his satisfaction, he turned to chronology. By carrying out a
program designed to reveal the sequence of superimposed geological layers at Lindenmeier, he was able to establish the stratigraphic chronology of the site. Later, one of the leading Pleistocene geologists of the day, Kirk Bryan, along with his student
Louis Ray, was able to correlate these strata with the surface
geomorphology of northeastern Colorado and to make estimates
of the site's age. Their estimate of 10,000 to 25,000 years was,
as we shall see, remarkably accurate.

The question of origins is more difficult. Any answer to it is
complicated by the fact that evidence, either in support or in
refutation, must be indirect and cannot be observed simply in
material associations at a site or in a sequence of superimposed
layers. It should be clear that a failure to appreciate this aspect
of the problem is implicit in all earlier attempts to answer the
question of Indian origins which were outlined in the previous
chapter.

A similar failure plagued Roberts; a failure accounted for by
then current notions about the distinctiveness of human racial
types and their geographic distribution. Anthropologists in the
1930s and 1940s recognized many more "races" and "stocks"
than they do now, and each of these racial types was assigned
its own location of development. Roberts and practically all of
his contemporaries who were concerned with Pleistocene man,
wherever found, thought that minor variations in skeletal form
indicated distinctive external features. Those phenotypic differences were thought to be the product of genetic selection
arising in isolated populations; they thus could provide direct
evidence of association with some parent group. Hence, it followed that American Indian origins would be known if such an
association could be demonstrated with Asian peoples. Of
course, no such association can be made. Variation within any
population is great and individual characteristics overlap with
those of other populations to such a degree that only the gross-
est distinctions between populations can be made with confidence. Roberts' search for origins did not differ in principle
from that of his sixteenth century predecessors.

Roberts' third question was thus badly put. Nonetheless, he went about searching for relevant evidence in a systematic and logically sound manner. He failed to find the desired skeletons, but in the search he uncovered and recorded a great deal of valuable information about the material remains of the Lindenmeier campsite that would otherwise have gone unnoticed. This information is now pertinent to an entirely different kind of problem centered on the question: How were Pleistocene hunting-gathering societies organized? My interest in Lindenmeier was stimulated by the discovery that this information exists. I believe that a partial answer to this new question can be given if a different interpretive strategy were applied to the Lindenmeier material.

My approach has had two related goals. The first is methodological and consists in searching for ways to extract data from a set of materials that are relevant to a search for organizational structure. The second is operational and directed toward the discovery of the nature and degree of variation in Lindenmeier artifact form and spacing. Before considering these two goals fully in the next chapter, I will outline briefly my data collection procedures.

First, I had to learn as much about the site as possible. Roberts kept meticulously detailed field records and from these it was possible to determine the specific place at which the great majority of specimens were found. As there are 1557 pages of field notes and catalogues as well as 287 pages of Smithsonian accession records and more than 200 storage trays full of specimens, it seemed far easier to reassemble the collection than to constantly search through these records for needed information. In essence, the site was recreated on a very large layout table by arranging rows and columns of boxes, each box representing one excavation square, and placing all of the artifacts in their appropriate boxes. Simultaneously, a parallel process took place as the information in Roberts' field notes was converted to useable locational data. Plots showing the distribution of specimens and stratigraphic profiles were drawn. Specimens for which inadequate information is available were not included; there were very few of these—less than 5 percent of the total inventory.

Stratigraphy

Having discussed the geological history of the Lindenmeier Valley earlier in this chapter, I can now turn to the stratigraphy of the site itself and to a consideration of the relations between the several clusters of occupation debris and a series of successively developed ground surfaces.

Recall for a moment the environment described: a small valley with its meandering stream flooding first one and then another depression in its floodplain. These well-watered areas supported luxuriant plant communities which, during repeated cycles of growth and decay, gradually filled the depressions with humic debris. As each area filled, its level with respect to the stream bed was raised and lower areas were, in turn, flooded. The entire valley floor was thus progressively elevated and the top of each filled depression was for a time, until the cycle repeated itself, the exposed ground surface of that area.

Periodically, the people living in the region made camps in the Lindenmeier Valley. They did so, of course, on then currently exposed ground surfaces. Camp debris—scraps of meals, waste products of manufacture, broken or lost tools—accumulated around the living area. Each surface was exposed for many years and, consequently, was repeatedly camped upon. Old camp areas sometimes were reused, but new camps were also established in previously unoccupied places. Through time, camps were established on a succession of surfaces (see Fig. 3.5b).

There is no way of knowing how much time elapsed between the establishment of the ground surfaces, but we can speak in terms of decades at least. However, we do know that all of the events took place about 11,000 years ago. Two radiocarbon ages have been determined for the site. One was obtained by Vance Haynes (Haynes and Agogino, 1964) from charcoal which he collected from an exposure of the black stratum in the modern arroyo bank. The age which he obtained is 10,780 ± 375 radiocarbon years—8820 B.C. Another age estimate was made by Geochron, Inc., from charcoal collected from a hearth by Roberts and submitted by me for analysis in 1967. This estimate is 11,200 ± 400 radiocarbon years—9250 B.C. The standard deviations of these age determinations overlap; there is thus no reason to assume that the ages are different. For convenience, I will use 11,000 years for the age of the site.

Site Units

When Roberts excavated at Lindenmeier, he found only the more decay-resistant remains of some of these camp debris accumulations. These materials occurred in clusters a few of which were clearly separated horizontally and vertically from others. However, most clusters overlap stratigraphically; that is, the surfaces upon which they lie are separated by such thin layers of soil that the material from two or more clusters is mixed. The spatially-distinct clusters may be identified with discrete camp areas, but the mixed ones cannot be completely segregated with certainty.

At least fifteen separate clusters are recognizable; their locations are diagrammed in Fig. 3.10. Of these, only five offer suitably complete information to repay extensive intracluster analysis. They are labeled Units A, B, F, G, and H on the figure. A, B, and most of F are clearly distinguishable. G and H are substantially intermingled but are in large measure separable. Only material from these five units will be used in the analyses which follow. Unit D (the Big Pit) and Unit E (the Bison Pit) plus the Coffin area assemblage were completely excavated and contained dense concentrations of artifacts, but collections from these areas were poorly recorded. Consequently, it is not possible to use material from these units. Unit C plus the areas marked 1, 2, and 3 were only partially excavated.

Let us now turn our attention to the segregation of the materials in Units G and H. A basis for assigning a reasonable number of specimens in mixed areas to their respective units is obtained by summing all specimens which occur at equal intervals of depth with respect to each former surface. If debris were deposited on only one surface, we should expect the distribution of material above and below that surface to take the form of a sharply peaked curve whose apex is at or near the surface depth (see Fig. 3.11a). Deviations from this form of distribution will indicate mixing of material from different levels. Specimens which occur within the overlapping distributional areas of two or more surfaces cannot be assigned to any occupation.

Table 3.3 tabulates the depths at which all specimens in two different areas were found; Figure 3.11b,c displays these data as frequency diagrams. Unit A is a spatially discrete cluster; its material is vertically distributed as predicted (compare Fig. 3.11b with Fig. 3.11a).

Units G and H (along with Unit I) partially overlap each other in an area of very thin strata (Fig. 3.11c). The vertical

——→

Fig. 3.10

Topographic map showing locations of excavated areas. A–I mark separate identifiable deposits; 1–6 mark less extensive excavations.

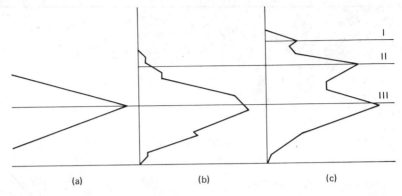

Fig. 3.11

Verticle distribution of artifacts with respect to occupied ground surfaces: (a) expected form of distribution frequency curve if only one surface occupied; (b) actual distribution in Unit A (surface II unoccupied); (c) actual distribution in area of overlap of Units G, H, I (surfaces I, II, III all occupied).

Table 3.3

Proportions of Artifacts Found at 1-inch Increments Above and Below Ancient Ground Surfaces.

DEPTH	UNIT A		UNITS G, H, I		
	SURFACE		SURFACE		
(INCHES)	I	II	I	II	III
+4	.005	.04	.005	.02	—
+3	.01	.07	.01	.02	.03
+2	.01	.07	.01	.07	.12
+1	.01	.08	.02	.11	.16
−1	.02	.09	.03	.09	.08
−2	.02	.10	.02	.08	.05
−3	.01	.08	.02	.03	.02
−4	.02	.05	—	—	.01

Table 3.4
Area Calculation for Occupation Units.

Unit	Gross	Net	Adjust	Total	Area (m²)
A	106	71	7	78	179
B	89	60	0	60	127
F	38	38	7	45	103
G	66	66	6	72	166
H	54	54	18	72	166

Gross = total number of excavated squares.
Net   = gross number of squares minus peripheral empty squares.
Adjust = estimate of unexcavated portion of unit.
Total = net plus adjust.

distribution of specimens in these units departs strongly from that predicted for single unit occupations. But notice that the modal peaks of the curve fall just below the average depth of the three surfaces and that the form of the curve near each peak is the same as it is for a single unadulterated distribution. It is clear that all three surfaces were camped upon. Unit I is underrepresented in the sample because excavation procedures were not designed to recover all the material above the black layers. The calculations and estimates are given in Table 3.2. The approximate areal extent and artifact density may now be estimated for the five units A, B, F, G, and H.

Unit Areas and Densities

A plan of specimen distribution found in Unit A is given in Fig. 3.12; Units B, F, G, and H are similar in appearance. Unit areas were calculated by counting the number of 5 × 5 foot excavation squares within each unit. For Units A and B, this total was reduced by disregarding those squares containing fewer than one standard deviation of the mean number of specimens per square for each unit. This was done to correct for scatter around the periphery of the actual living spaces of these unconfined locations. Squares with specimen densities equal to or less than $5/m^2$ were eliminated by this procedure; the remaining area contained 90 percent of all specimens in each unit. This reduction correction was not applied to Units F,

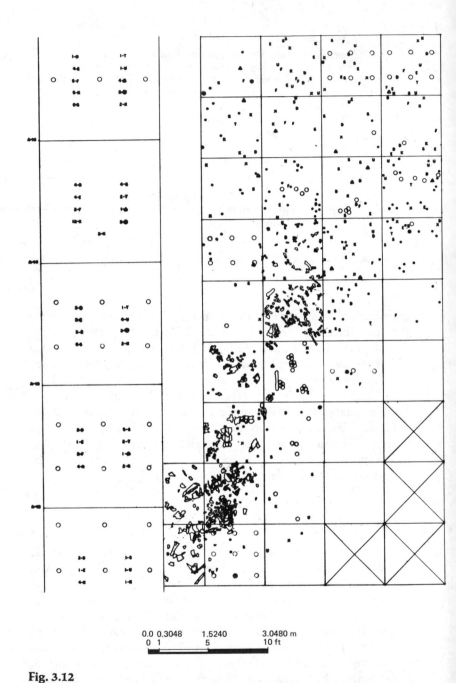

0.0	0.3048	1.5240	3.0480 m
0	1	5	10 ft

Fig. 3.12

Distribution plot of Unit A. The large squares are part of Trench A; each measures 10 ft. on a side. The smaller squares are 5 ft. on a side. Squares with x's are not included in the analysis because they either contained too few specimens or were stratigraphically mixed.

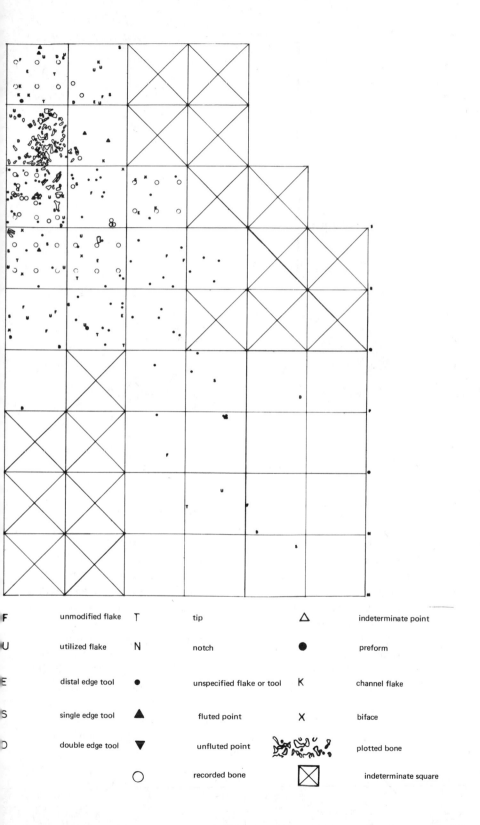

F	unmodified flake	T	tip	△	indeterminate point
U	utilized flake	N	notch	●	preform
E	distal edge tool	•	unspecified flake or tool	K	channel flake
S	single edge tool	▲	fluted point	X	biface
D	double edge tool	▼	unfluted point		plotted bone
		○	recorded bone	⊠	indeterminate square

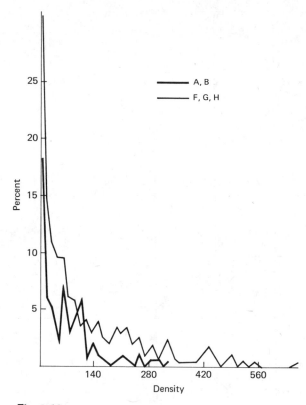

Fig. 3.13

Proportion of excavated squares containing specified numbers of artifacts.

G, and H because they contained no low density squares, and thus their limits were probably not reached by excavation. Next, adjustments were made to compensate for unexcavated portions of each unit and areas were calculated. The results are given in Table 3.4. Areas vary between 180m² for Unit A and 103m² for Unit F; mean area per unit is 148m².

Artifact density was calculated by dividing the total number of artifacts found in each net unit area by the number of square meters in that area; tool densities vary between 22/m² and 74/m². The density of chipping debris is plotted in Fig. 3.13.

At the end of several months of following this procedure, I was at a point equivalent to having just completed excavation of the site, seeing it lying open with everything in place, and ready to begin analyzing the collection.

Next a series of measurements for 10 variables and notations for 14 attributes were made for each specimen.* These data were coded for computer manipulation and used to test a series of hypotheses about site contents. The relationship of Lindenmeier to a broader system of sites was then considered.

REFERENCES

Bryan, Kirk, and Louis Ray
    1940   Geological antiquity of the Lindenmeier site in Colorado. *Smithsonian Miscellaneous Collections*, Vol. 99, No. 2.
Coffin, Roy G.
    1937   *Northern Colorado's First Settlers*. Reprinted by Department of Geology, Colorado State University.
Haynes, C. Vance, and George Agogino
    1964   Geological significance of a new radiocarbon date from the Lindenmeier site. *Denver Museum of Natural History, Proceedings*, No. 9.
Hrdlička, Aleš
    1925   The origin and antiquity of the American Indian. *Smithsonian Annual Report for 1923*, pp. 481–495.
    1932   The coming of man from Asia in the light of recent discoveries. *American Philosophical Society, Proceedings*, Vol. 71, pp. 393–402.
Kidder, Alfred V.
    1936   Speculations on New World prehistory. *Essays in Anthropology Presented to A. L. Kroeber*, R. H. Lowie (ed.), pp. 143–152. Berkeley, University of California Press.
Kroeber, Alfred L.
    1940   Conclusions: The present status of Americanist problems. In *The Maya and Their Neighbors*, C. L. Hay and others (eds.), pp. 460–487. New York, Appleton-Century.
MacCurdy, George G. (ed.)
    1937   *Early Man*. Philadelphia and New York, Lippincott.
Roberts, Frank H. H., Jr.
    1935   A Folsom complex: Preliminary report on investigations at the Lindenmeier site in northern Colorado. *Smithsonian Miscellaneous Collections*, Vol. 94, No. 4.
    1936   Additional information on the Folsom complex. *Smithsonian Miscellaneous Collections*, Vol. 95, No. 10.
    1940   Excavations at the Lindenmeier site contribute new information on the Folsom complex. *Explorations and Field-Work of the Smithsonian Institution in 1939*, pp. 87–92.

*Variables are measured; attributes are counted. (See pp. 62–63.)

4. A Structure for Investigation

Roberts and his associates worked in a strictly classificatory framework of interpretation. The types—of artifacts, of animals, of places—which they established were mutually exclusive classes into which individual items were fitted. Time, too, was chopped into discrete sequential segments.

CLASSIFICATION

Classification is a dividing process by which phenomena are segregated according to preestablished criteria. Classes are defined by certain distinctive traits. Individual items are assigned to a particular class if they have the defining traits for that class. A class, thus, is an either-or pigeonhole into which an item does or does not fit.

Yet, class difinitions often are changed: When a new set of items is typologically divided for the first time, classes are usually defined by a few readily apparent traits only. The range of variation in these traits usually increases as more of these items come to light. It becomes increasingly difficult to fit *all* items into the initial classes for the same reason that it is difficult to separate absolutely 'white' objects from 'black' objects when a series of grey objects, finely graded from nearly white to nearly black, is present. To overcome this difficulty, the original class system is expanded, more traits are added to class definitions, and the number of classes is increased. The principle of division into mutually exclusive categories is retained; items already classified along with subsequently discovered items are simply fitted into the newly formed classes according to more restrictive criteria.

This process of classification is well illustrated by the history of fluted point nomenclature as it developed during the first quarter-century after the Folsom discovery. The most obviously distinctive characteristic of the projectile points found at Folsom is a shallowly concave channel that extends along the central axis of one or both faces of a specimen (see Fig. 2.2). Correspondingly, the class 'fluted (or grooved) point' was informally established, and points with the definitive trait 'shallowly concave channel' were assigned to this class.

It was soon noticed, however, that not all fluted points were otherwise alike. Two classes, Folsom and Folsom-like, were defined to accommodate the observed differences: Folsom-like points were distinguished by generally greater size, usually less delicate chipping, and relatively shorter, more narrow flutes. Subsequently, as the number of known specimens increased, the Folsom-like category was abandoned in favor of a new series of named classes for each of which a criterion of shape was added to those already defined. The resultant classes are still used today; they include Clovis, Cumberland, Redstone, and other major divisions of fluted points.

Another aspect of this classificatory subdivision must be mentioned. Some points share all the essential Folsom class traits except flutes; these specimens have been assigned to a separate class labeled Midland or, sometimes, unfluted Folsom. Another assigned class of points, Plainview, extensively overlaps the Clovis class, but again, this class is fluteless although many specimens show a type of flaking which to some observers appears to be partial fluting.

The weakness inherent in all typologies of the classificatory sort is well exemplified in the above outline. Furthermore, a critical weakness of this particular scheme should be apparent. Objects such as projectile points often cannot be neatly pigeonholed in the manner illustrated. Those traits which appear to be most diagnostic of a class often are not easily assessed by simple presence or absence decisions.

Fluting, dimensions of size, and other traits definitive of fluted point classes are among those that cannot be so assessed. It follows that a large number of individual specimens will not fit well into any class, or rather, they will fit partially into several classes. The resultant classification will either exhibit a large miscellaneous class and, thus, admit its shortcomings, or more likely, it will contain not classes but mixed collections of items. Variation within these categories will be nearly as great as it is between categories. Fluted point classes are mixed assortments of the latter kind. Many archaeologists have recognized these shortcomings, but no satisfactory solution has been proposed.

The construction of class typologies is reasonable when the goal of investigation is to segregate phenomena. In this, Paleo-Indian classifications served their purpose well for they were developed to satisfy a desire to divide space, time, and prehistory into separate units. Roberts, and others who worked in this field, were consistent in their approach—artifacts and sites were typologically classified in similar ways. Paleo-Indian remains, like other archaeological remains, were thought to be adequately explained if they could be placed in appropriate classes. But placement in a class is simply a form of description and no more. These typologies, thus, were ends in themselves rather than means to an end.

UNIQUENESS

The underlying assumption of archaeological class division has been one of individual uniqueness. This notion has been transferred to classes which are then treated as if they were discrete entities with objective realities of their own. This view is encapsulated in most textbooks on prehistory: A type specimen is selected to represent a whole class of objects; thereafter, the type serves as the unit of study and comparison.

Variations among specimens within a class have been ignored. Each member of a class is considered to be equivalent to the "type specimen" which, in turn, is treated as the standard of reference when other specimens are compared. This bizarre situation arose because there is no way to measure degree of flutedness or Folsomness or other such quality. As the methodological goal was to compartmentalize, the obvious thing to do was to create the abstract classes, 'fluted point,' 'Folsom,' and so forth and to grant unique status to each.

But uniqueness, far from being an inherent property of things, lies in the eye of the beholder. If we adhere to a view of uniqueness we limit ourselves to considering only the obvious; we will, accordingly, be able to say only "each thing is as it is."

Postan's often quoted sketch makes the same point: Newton, after being hit on his head by an apple falling from its tree, rejected the unique in favor of a general view of things:

> Had he asked himself the obvious question: why did that particular apple choose that unrepeatable instant to fall on that unique head, he might have written the history of an apple. Instead of which he asked himself why apples fall and produced the theory of gravitation. (1948:409)

Similarly, if we ask not what is unique about a site or an artifact—or a class of these—but rather what regularities exist among a set of sites or artifacts, we can then consider them to be individual cases that fit, at some potentially knowable point, into the range of variation of all the cases. We have no trouble in viewing familiar items in this way: Among automobiles we recognize many different brands, but we do not therefore *isolate* Fords from Cadillacs. Instead, we are able to consider automobiles in terms of differences in models, capacity, speed, function, and so forth, and have no difficulty in recognizing Henry's Ford as being simply another car rather than something special.

CONNECTIONS

Clearly, the dimensions of our category 'automobile' have many axes, some of which differentiate physical properties (e.g., engine size) and some conceptual properties (e.g., notions of status). Most people are able to connect these axes intuitively although most will not be able to give a systematic account of their connectivity. For the past, however, we do not have this kind of intuitive knowledge; yet we wish to arrive at some understanding—some systematic idealization or account—of past events. To reach such an understanding, the observable physical characteristics of our subject material (sites and artifacts) must be connected in a model with at least some conceptual terms which encompass these characteristics. That is, rather than compartmentalize according to differentiating criteria, we need to specify characteristics of our material along many axes and formulate some hypotheses about relations between them.

Such specifications cannot be made in terms of observed morphological traits alone. Again, were we to limit ourselves to such specifications we would be restricted to examining relations between obvious physical properties, and the often voiced stricture that archaeologists cannot "put flesh on the dry bones" of their material would continue to hold. If, to extend the automobile analogy, we were to consider cars solely in terms of their external appearances, we would undoubtedly devise some class ordering that would compartmentalize automobiles in an appropriate chronological sequence, for it is true that 1929 Fords and 1929 Cadillacs resemble each other more than either resembles its 1969 counterpart. Furthermore, upon examining the internal parts of automobiles we would find that a similar ordering would hold: Ignition systems, engines, transmission systems, and so forth, were more similar among all 1929 brands than between any pair of 1929 and 1969 models. In other words, regardless of the number of axes measured, if they all measure only physical properties we will still be able to do no more than catalogue and classify. The situation would be similar to that which characterizes present fluted point classifications.

But there are other things about automobiles that are important. Among these are relational questions such as "why are all 1929 automobiles more like each other than they are like those of 1969?" We can easily list the traits that describe the conditions of likeness and unlikeness, but to answer the question "Why . . . ?" we must refer to concepts which underlie scientific discoveries, industrial inventions, innovations in applied chemistry and metallurgy, "car-of-the-future" design contests, and the growth of unionism, as well as to other independent concepts which encompass aspects of automobile manufacture. For example, changes in the chemistry of gasoline composition has been accompanied by changes in engine production and this has led to a series of systematic changes in the entire power train of automobiles. All brands are more-or-less simultaneously affected and, thus, all change through time in roughly equivalent ways.

Now consider the fact that automobiles manufactured in 1969 were rarely painted black but that almost all 1929 cars were black. We could, of course, construct a class 'black automobiles' and another 'kandy-kolored tangerine-flake streamline babies' (a parallel procedure is often followed by those who work with prehistoric pottery). But to do so would be, again, to mask the most important aspects of the variation. We could, alternatively, construct an empirical hypothesis that predicts a causal relation between the availability of paints of adequate durability and the color of cars and find that, while suitable candy-colored paints were not widely available in 1929, black paints of high quality continue to be available in 1969. Neither this nor any other hypothesis that specifies a purely technological cause for the colors of automobiles can be confirmed. A more complete explanation must be sought in other directions which certainly involve social and psychological factors.

The fact that buggies drawn by horses were most commonly black is relevant; the process by which the characteristic 'blackness' was transferred to horseless carriages must be taken into consideration. Furthermore, the fact that certain kinds of cars— the Stutz Bearcat was one—were usually not black, in fact were often yellow, suggests that some factor other than a purely technological one was at work. Every reader of this book intuitively understands that reappearance in the 1970s of black as a popular color on automobiles—first on "muscle cars" and always in combination with bright colors—is not a technological phenomenon. But to explain the basis of this understanding, a whole series of conceptual properties must be called upon.

Methodologically, what is important in the foregoing discussion is the implication that observable attributes, while they contribute data for testing relations between different properties of a set of materials, are not themselves tested. To test such relations it will be necessary to specify a set of conceptual characteristics for the subject materials, formulate a set of hypotheses in terms of these characteristics, and assign empirical attributes to them which may be applied in tests of the hypotheses already formulated.

If, for example, a set of relations between the penetrating effectiveness of projectile points, the rigidity of their attachment to shafts, different techniques for affecting these attachments, and cross-sectional shapes of points were specified, then it would be possible to determine the conditions under which a fluted point would be one alternative form for adequately satisfying the specified relations.

After the attributes conditioned by these technological and functional constraints have been defined, a set of shape and flaking attributes that are essentially independent of these constraints may remain. The finishing retouch around the edges of points is an example. To explain this remaining variation, it will be necessary to formulate a specific set of relations between, say, the division of societies into subunits (e.g., families, bands, tribes), the localization of such subunits, the processes of transmitting information to successive generations, and functionally-independent variation in projectile points. In addition, it will be necessary to specify a set of empirical implications of these relations, such as some predictions about the spatial distributions of attributes under consideration.

This procedure does not lead to a series of classes or types. A specimen may be analyzed in one set of dimensions according to its technological composition and in quite another stylistically. Attributes and variables are attached to independent conceptual characteristics and their significance deduced by hypothesis from these. Black cars are, thus, not handled simply as cars that are black, but to their blackness is attached a meaning that is conceptually independent of the category 'cars.' Similarly, fluted points and other archaeological specimens should neither be treated as separate, differentiated objects nor as constricted class phenomena. If we are to unravel the threads of prehistory, we must look upon artifacts and sites as mosaics of attributes and variables which are tied to different characteristics of cultural systems. A procedure for treating artifacts in this way will be developed in the next chapter, and this will be followed by considerations for treating sites as parts of spatial systems.

THEORIES AND MODELS

A theory is a system of interlocking statements about relations between certain defined phenomena. From a theory it is possible to deduce observable consequences of the specified relations and, in this manner, to account for observed phenomena. As Hanson (1965:90) has said, "Theories provide patterns within which data appear intelligible." Many philosophers of science argue that it is impossible to observe anything in a conceptual vacuum; they mean by this that we observe things in the context of our perceptions of the world.

If, for example, I see a set of letters that I call a "word," then I already have the abstract concept 'semantic unit' in my conceptual frame of reference. And although I can neither speak nor read a single word of Czech, I can easily transfer my ability to recognize English word units and pick out Czech words on a printed page with essentially 100 percent success. I can do this because English and Czech position letters into words according to the same set of principles and because I know what those principles are. But if I am confronted with a page of Chinese, I cannot pick out words because I am not familiar with the rules for writing Chinese.

The point is that to make sense of observations—indeed, in order to observe particular entities at all—we must have guidelines to direct and give form to our observations. In science, this conceptual guidance is provided by a body of theory. Perhaps the easiest way to clarify this relationship between theory and observed phenomena is through a series of diagrams.

Let us assign the following equivalencies:

$$T = \text{Theory}$$

$$M = \text{Model}$$

$$O = \text{Observable}$$

There are, of course, many possible Ts, many possible Ms, and many possible Os. We may consider the relations between them in the two ways shown in Figs. 4.1 and 4.2.

These figures have in common the fact that models act as a bridge between theoretical conceptions and the observables to be connected to them. The nature of models will be considered in a moment; for the present purpose it is only necessary to notice that they act as intermediaries between theories and observable sense phenomena. But here the commonality between the figures ends.

Figure 4.1 diagrams an inductive procedure by means of which attempts are made to attach observables directly to models and models to theories by working upward. Working in this direction leads to uncertain results because there is no way to connect lower levels to specific points in higher levels without running the risk of creating a needless repetition (tautology). In other words, if we attempt to say that O_1 is a case of M_1 because we have placed O_1 in M_1, we have stated a circular argument. Looking for the appropriate M for each O is similar to looking for *the* bolt from which a nut found on the street has been lost. After lengthy search, *a* bolt which fits the nut may be found, but it will not be known whether it is the bolt in question.

Figure 4.2 diagrams a deductive approach. T statements are established; models (M) are constructed which predict empirical consequences of these T statements; the predictions specify the observables (O) that are relevant. We are thus guided in our search for data. For example, if I find a nut missing from the

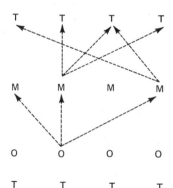

Fig. 4.1

Diagram of inductive reasoning. The broken arrows indicate uncertainty in the connections.

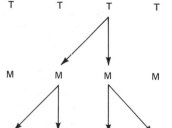

Fig. 4.2

Diagram of deductive reasoning. The solid arrows indicate that the connecting links are guided by higher levels of inclusion.

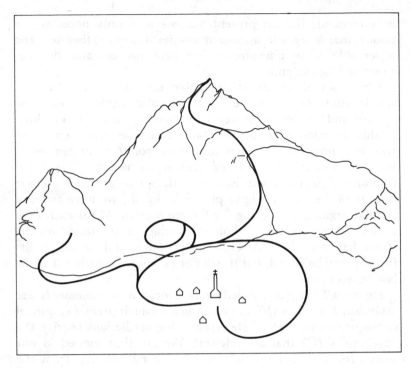

Fig. 4.3

Paths on a mountain. The diagram has been highly simplified; nonetheless, if you imagine yourself to be very small and moving along the path, the choices to make in order to reach the top would by no means be clear.

toaster in my kitchen, I will probably begin to search for it in the kitchen and not elsewhere. When I find a nut that fits, other information—its color, shape, whether it matches other nuts on the toaster—will reinforce my confidence that I have the missing nut.

Another way of looking at the difference between inductive and deductive reasoning is by an illustration (Fig. 4.3). If I am in a village at the bottom of a mountain and wish to reach the mountaintop, I can start walking on any path leading from the village. But unless I know which of many paths leads to the top I will probably go to many deadends or perhaps walk around in circles. If, on the other hand, I am able to start at the top of the mountain and walk down, I will be better able to judge which is the correct downward path. I will be able to do this because I will have an overview of the entire structure of the mountain and will be better able to predict which path decision will most likely lead me to the village. A knowledge of geomorphology and mountaineering would further help reduce the number of false turns that I might make. A topographic map, if available, could be used to check my bearings from time to time. In this illustration, prior knowledge (of geomorphology and mountaineering) stands in the place of theory, and the map is equivalent to a model. The map (model), of course, can serve equally well when walking upward, but it cannot be drawn until the structure (theory) of the mountain is known. Once the path has been delineated, I can easily go in either direction.

Now let us consider the relationship between theory, model, and observables in a somewhat more specific way.

T (conceptual framework)	includes statements about such mechanical properties as rigidity, friction, adhesion
M (translation of T in terms of O)	a. operational procedures for controlling rigidity between parts of projectiles (spears, arrows, etc.) are defined, and so on b. relevant variables and attributes are specified c. hypotheses setting forth different values for the terms of (b) under alternative conditions of (a) are formulated
O (observables)	includes observations about a. projectile points (p) o_{p_1} = fluted forms o_{p_2} = lanceolate forms . . . o_{p_n} = n-shaped forms b. distribution (d) o_{d_1} = "fluted points are restricted in space" . . . o_{d_n} = "fluted points are everywhere"

The argument can be stated as follows: In the absence of adhesives and fasteners, friction must be the sole binding force between a point and a haft. If friction is the binding agent, it is advantageous, for any constant binding pressure, to increase the area of surface contact between parts. This may be done in two ways: First, by increasing the size of the surfaces in contact and second, by increasing the smoothness of contacting surfaces. If friction is the principal binding agent, we should expect to find points with large, flat surfaces on both faces.

Fluted points have just such surfaces. We may deduce that fluting was developed in accordance with the mechanical requirements—in the absence of adhesives—for effecting the firm attachment of a point to the end of a spear or javelin. This explanation also offers a plausible reason for the fact that fluted points are limited to North America and the northern parts of Latin America. When the Americas were colonized from Asia, a vast area of treeless tundra was passed through and, therefore, pinepitch and other vegetable mastics would be unknown to generations of hunters. Friction was thus the most readily available holding agent. It also can account for the scarcity of bifacial projectile points in the Eurasian Paleolithic and Mesolithic since coniferous adhesives were always available with which simple shapes could be attached to hafts. Further, a reason for the short-lived history of fluted points is suggested; these are highly inefficient tools. They break easily when being made and during use; consequently, they would be replaced by stronger points shortly after coniferous resins were again available and their adhesive properties rediscovered.

Now consider the following from which we legitimately deduce that fluted points are unique and that it is proper to group them into units of uniqueness.

T (conceptual framework)   includes the statement "things are unique"

M (translation   'things' is given an operational of T in terms of O)   definition
'uniqueness' is given an operational definition

O (observables) $o_{p_1} =$ fluted points
$o_{p_2} =$ lanceolate points
.
.
.
$o_{p_n} =$ n-shaped points

Some weaknesses of the concept of uniqueness have already
been discussed, and the present illustration underscores the fact
that our conceptions structure our observations.

ANALOGIES

Analogical models describe something unfamiliar in terms of
something more familiar. They are intended to bring the unknown into the realm of our ordinary experience so that we may
more easily envision its nature. Analogies do not explain unknown phenomena; they simply interpret some parts of those
phenomena in language that we understand. Thus, an analogy
in science is like a metaphor in literature in that it associates
vague ideas and entities with others that are already concretely
established. And like a metaphor, an analogical model may suggest extension of the described relations and, thereby, lead to
other unsuspected relations between phenomena. It is in this
that analogical models have their greatest value.

Reference to automobiles to illustrate the processes and consequences of classification as applied to fluted point typologies
is such an analogy. I intend by it to make clear that archaeological classification has had the same syntactic structure (that
is, the same way of ordering its parts) as does our usual division
of automobile makes and models—and, by extension, our usual
compartmentalization of the everyday items of our experience.
The parts that are ordered, in all these cases, are traits, classes,
and specimens; the order into which the parts are placed resembles a series of pigeonholes or boxes, each separate from
the others.

ORDERINGS AND EXPLANATIONS

The box analogy is useful to illuminate the nature of classifying
typologies as well as some ways in which these typologies
are used to explain archaeological phenomena. Let us say that
the notation $\{A, B, C, \ldots, n\}$ represents a set of archaeological
phenomena (a set of artifacts, of sites, or any other set of
archaeological things). The members of a set will be called
events. It is possible to think of these events in a number of
ways. The following diagrams represent some of these pos-
sibilities:

$$\boxed{A} \quad \boxed{B} \quad \boxed{C} \quad \ldots \quad \boxed{n} \; . \qquad (4.1)$$

This is simply a graphic translation of the box analogy in

which $\boxed{A}$ stands for one class, $\boxed{B}$ for another, and so forth through $\boxed{n}$, which is the last class. Let (4.1) stand for a *cataloging model* of the kind discussed in the first half of this chapter. In it, "Folsom point" might be substituted for $\mathbf{A}$, "Clovis point" for $\mathbf{C}$, and so forth. The order of substitution is of no importance so long as the defining traits of each box are not violated.

Other models are easily derived from this one. They may be diagrammed as follows:

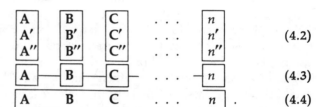

$$
\begin{array}{cccc}
\boxed{\begin{array}{c}A\\A'\\A''\end{array}} & \boxed{\begin{array}{c}B\\B'\\B''\end{array}} & \boxed{\begin{array}{c}C\\C'\\C''\end{array}} & \begin{array}{c}\cdot\;\cdot\;\cdot\\\cdot\;\cdot\;\cdot\\\cdot\;\cdot\;\cdot\end{array} & \boxed{\begin{array}{c}n\\n'\\n''\end{array}} & (4.2)
\end{array}
$$

$$
\boxed{A}\!-\!\boxed{B}\!-\!\boxed{C}\!- \;\cdot\;\cdot\;\cdot\; -\!\boxed{n} \qquad (4.3)
$$

$$
\boxed{\begin{array}{ccccc}A & B & C & \cdots & n\end{array}}\;. \qquad (4.4)
$$

Of these, (4.2) depicts a *comparative model*. A model of this kind is merely an extension of descriptive class models like (4.1). In them, events are grouped by ordering defined classes according to whether they are more like $\mathbf{A}$ or $\mathbf{B}$ or n. The division of fluted points into several named types—Folsom, Clovis, Cumberland, etc.—follows this procedure.

Next, let (4.3) stand for a *simple sequence model*. This model orders the classes of (4.1) into a series on which the order of placement is important. Thus, questions of whether fluted points are earlier than unfluted points or whether Clovis is earlier than Folsom become relevant. According to present estimates based on radiocarbon dating, the proper Paleo-Indian sequence is $\boxed{A}$ = Clovis, $\boxed{B}$ = Folsom, $\boxed{C}$ = unfluted points (e.g., Plainview). It is obvious that simple sequence models are meant to tell more about events than are classifying models. But the additional information is entirely descriptive: Placement in time is a part of the description of an event just as is placement in space.

Diagram (4.4) represents a *developmental model*. Such models attempt more than description because they suggest that one stage of a sequence developed from the preceding stage. Each stage is accounted for in part as a continuation of its predecessor and in part by a description of new traits which are characteristic of it. A stage, thus, is linked to the immediately preceding one because it contains traits that are reasonably expectable given the presence of certain similar traits in the earlier stage. For example, even before radiocarbon age estimates were available, Folsom points were placed in a developmental sequence after Clovis points because the former have finer, more regular flaking and longer, more shallow flutes than do the latter.

But even developmental models consider only a few of the properties of the cultural events under study; furthermore, they focus on only those facts which are most readily observed. All these models consider only the events themselves and ignore those properties which form the events. They are, thus, limited to answering simple questions of What and Where; if a sequential scale can be applied, they also are able to answer questions of When. But none can offer explanations of the events—questions of How and Why must go unasked. To answer questions of this kind, a more inclusive model is needed.

An explanatory model assumes that different characteristics of a set of events are interdependent rather than separately classifiable. Observable properties of these events are connected to conceptual terms by hypotheses and specific consequences of the model can in this way be tested. A model of this kind may be called a *theoretical model* because it connects observables to theoretical concepts by means of a systematic series of hypotheses. It may be diagrammed:

$$\bar{A} <\!\!> A <\!\!> \underline{A} \quad AB \quad \bar{B} <\!\!> B <\!\!> \underline{B} \quad B\underline{n} \quad \ldots \quad \bar{n} <\!\!> n <\!\!> \underline{n}.$$

$$(4.5)$$

where: $\bar{A}$ represents events other than A and which affect A, $\underline{A}$ represents events other than A and affected by A, etc.

This model has advantages over (4.1)–(4.4) because it considers not only events but also properties which define the events. Double arrows are used to indicate that influence is at least in part reciprocal. With this model, we can investigate the conditions under which A is a product of $\bar{A}$ and those by which $\underline{A}$ is derived from A. The specification of certain technological and functional conditions which might lead to the fluting of projectile points outlines an application of theoretical models. A more complex model of this kind will be presented in Chapter 5.

REFERENCES

Hanson, Norwood R.
  1965 *Patterns of Discovery*. Cambridge, Cambridge University Press.

Hempel, Carl G.
1966 *Philosophy of Natural Science.* Englewood Cliffs, N.J.,
Prentice-Hall.
Kuhn, Thomas
1970 *The Structure of Scientific Revolutions,* 2nd edition.
Chicago, University of Chicago Press.
Postan, M.
1948 The revulsion from thought. *Cambridge Journal.* Vol.
1, pp. 395–408.
Wolfe, Tom
1965 *The Kandy-Kolored, Tangerine-Flake, Streamline Baby.*
New York, Farrar, Straus & Giroux.

5. An Application of the Method

In this chapter, data are presented for application to the problem-oriented approach just discussed. The reasons for describing these data in the particular manner chosen are embedded in that approach and founded on the assumption that data exist only in relation to problems. A distinction must be made, therefore, between observations and data, first as general categories and second, as this distinction pertains to the Lindenmeier collection.

THE NATURE OF OBSERVATIONS

Observations are made through the direct sense perception of phenomena. Data are abstracted from observations; that is, they arise from the proposition that there is some connection between a particular set of observed phenomena and a conceived reason for their existence. Data are thus conceptually organized observations.

The form taken by such organization depends upon the context in which the information at hand is viewed. For example, we are informed that so-and-so many artifacts were observed here and there at Lindenmeier. But this information becomes data only in terms of questions such as, "Does this location differ from surrounding locations in the characteristic 'presence of artifacts'?" In other words, "Is this an archaeological site?" You will recognize that this is precisely the form taken by Roberts' first work at Lindenmeier. We are also informed exactly where most of the artifacts were found. Data pertinent to an investigation of stratigraphic chronology were generated from this information. Notions of differential distribution and principles of stratigraphy were well established and differences in the horizontal and vertical positions of assemblages could be investigated in terms of these.

It is probably clear now that failure to answer questions about origins lay more in an inability to convert archaeological observations into data appropriate to those questions than in the fact that human skeletal remains were absent from Lindenmeier. The conceptual framework available at the time did not provide an adequate guide for such conversion. It is noteworthy that Roberts made no attempt to expand, on the basis of material recovered during the last five years of his work, the answers to his first two questions. He correctly considered the collections made during those years—they amount to 85 percent of the total excavated assemblage—redundant to those questions.

Solutions to the problems inherent in long-range connections remain elusive in archaeology, but by altering our approach to the Lindenmeier assemblage in the manner suggested in the foregoing chapter, data relevant to an understanding of the organization of hunting societies can be defined. To generate appropriate data, it will be necessary:

1. To propose a set of connections between some physical characteristics of the Lindenmeier assemblage and some set of underlying conceptual properties which pertain to *all* assemblages and sites containing stone tools;
2. To formulate a set of hypotheses according to these;
3. To specify those empirical regularities to be expected among locations that are organized in the particular manner under consideration;
4. To demonstrate, by applying data to these hypotheses, that Lindenmeier is a specific case that falls within the predicted range of variation for sites so organized.

Data are defined in Step 3 when certain observations are given meaning in terms of the hypotheses of Step 2. In other words, those observations relevant to the propositions of Step 1 are isolated from the total possible information contained in the assemblage. This is a crucial step but one that is often overlooked. Observable traits to be compared are usually chosen because they are readily distinguished from others; they are seldom construed as interlocking components of a system. That is, "diagnostic" traits are segregated from other observable phenomena rather than connected to them by the set of common characteristics proposed in the initial stages of investigation. Roberts' search for skeletons is a case in point.

Fluted points have replaced bones as the prime indicator of commonality between Paleo-Indian locations, but no attempts have ever been made to show that the presence of fluting is either a necessary or a sufficient condition of commonality.

Moreover, no attempts have been made to connect the process of fluting to other flaking processes, or for that matter, to any other aspect of Paleo-Indian assemblages. The logical issue and the operational one are related; to deal with one, we must deal with the other. But fluted points and waste flakes cannot be compared typologically or even trait by trait. To treat these different categories of objects together, we can consider only those common properties which underlie their different physical shapes.

THE MEANING OF VARIATION

Let us now consider these properties. To begin with, it is obvious that artifacts vary greatly in appearance. To underscore that fact, a series of artifacts representing several broad categories is depicted in Fig. 5.1. Recall from the preceeding chapter the argument that if we concentrate our attention on obvious differences—in size, shape, color, or other characteristics—we will be left to contemplate only the uniqueness of specimens. But if the concept of variation is introduced into our consideration, we can treat specimens as alternative individual expressions of commonly held characteristics rather than as separate entities.

Let us understand by the term 'variation' a property applying only to differences that can be measured on the same scale. In so doing, we simply recognize the long standing realization that apples and oranges cannot be compared directly. There is no variation between apples and oranges; they are simply different. To compare these different things, we must construe them on scales for such things as roundness, softness, sugar content, specific gravity, and so forth. Variation is associated with properties of objects rather than with objects themselves.

Consequently, variation among artifacts is not simply the sum of a number of unique events but is rather the product of a series of processes that participate in the shaping of artifacts.

$\longrightarrow$

Fig. 5.1

A series of tools from Lindenmeier: (a) distal edge tool; (b) distal edge tool with steep lateral edge retouch; (c) notched tool; (d) blade with used edges; (e) double edge tool; (f) engraving tip; (g) single edge tool; (h) utilized flake. e is 78 mm long.

(a)

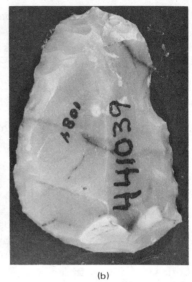

(b)

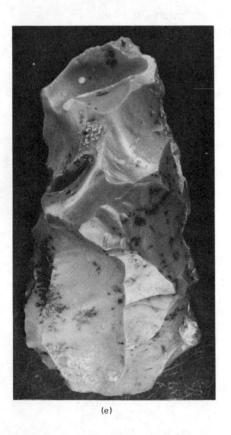

(e)

(f)

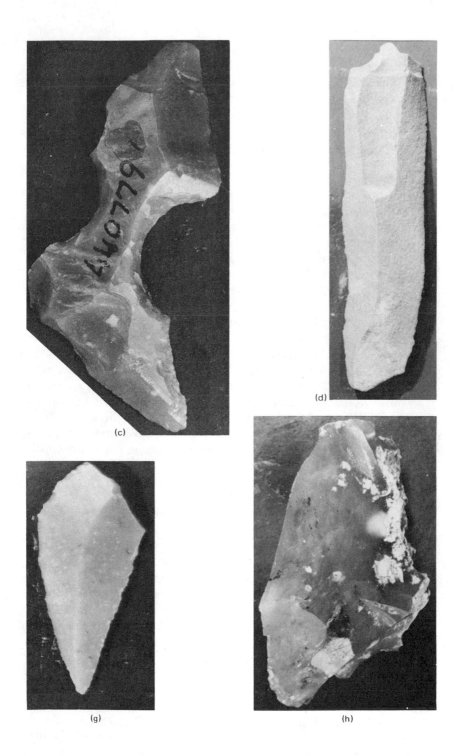

(c)

(d)

(g)

(h)

Processes which are common to artifacts of greatly differing shapes or categories will produce common characteristics on all specimens on which they operate. Even specimens of extremely divergent appearance (for example, a Folsom point and a small unused chip) may share certain features and hence, for purposes of investigating these, must be treated as variant cases of a common process. Other characteristics will be associated exclusively with a single artifact category. In order to assess the meaning of differences between sets of specimens, we must be able to account deductively for the variations among them in terms of causal processes which underlie specific characteristics.

Implied in the above discussion is the notion that variation is relative to the context of investigation. Differences that are purely mechanical in nature are significant data in a consideration of artifact production and use but are unlikely to be relevant to studies of, for instance, social processes—for these latter, such differences are merely differences.

Scales for measuring variation may be numerical and have a logical order from smallest to largest value; that is, 1 is smaller than 2 which is smaller than 3 and so forth to n, which is the largest. Such scales are called quantitative; the quantities measured are called variables. Examples of quantitative scales are those which measure length in millimeters or angles in degrees. Attributes are recorded on descriptive scales in which some symbol or numerical code stands for a specified quality but does not measure that quality; for instance, Clovis might arbitrarily be designated 1, Folsom 2, etc. Examples of attributes are those which code the different forms of edge retouch on points or the position of maximum width of flakes.

To describe the data in a useful manner, the distribution of values in a set of observations must be considered. Measures of central tendency (that describe average values) and of dispersion (that describe clustering around the average) will be used for this purpose. The measures are shown superimposed on the upper drawing of Fig. 5.12. For variables, the *mean* $(\bar{X})$ is the center of distribution of values; it is simply the arithmetic average of all the values. For both variables and attributes, the *mode* (M) defines the single interval into which most values fall. But these average measures, alone, do not give a clear picture of the nature of a distribution. Consider that two samples of five observations with values 10, 10, 10, 10, 10 and 0, 5, 10, 15, 20 respectively have the same means $(\bar{X}_1 = 10; \bar{X}_2 = 10)$. $M_1 = 10$, but M_2 has no value since all intervals have an equal number of observations. To get a true picture of the distribution, it is necessary also to look at measures of dispersion. One of these is the *range* (R) which describes the limits of observed measurements from a minimum to a maximum value. In the first example, $R_1 = 10$–10; in the second, $R_2 = 0$–20. Another measure of dispersion for variables is the *standard deviation* (s) which may be loosely described as the average deviation of each observation from its mean. In the examples, $s_1 = 0$ and $s_2 = 7.87$, respectively. About 68 percent of all measurements of a single phenomenon fall within one standard deviation of the mean.*

Use of these summary statistics allows a set of specimens to be described accurately without listing every measurement. Two or more sets of observations may also be readily compared.

DEFINITIONS

To prepare for an examination of the Lindenmeier material, we must now specify the empirical characteristics and theoretical properties with which we will be concerned. For convenience

*The computations of $\bar{X}$ and s are simple although for large samples they become tedious if done by hand. The basic formulas are

$$\bar{X} = \frac{\Sigma x}{N} \text{ and } s = \sqrt{\frac{\Sigma(x - \bar{X})^2}{N-1}}.$$

For $\bar{X}$, the observations (x) are summed and divided by the number of observations (N). For s, the difference of each observation from its mean is squared and all resultant products are summed. The total is divided by the number of observations minus one. The square root of the quotient is extracted. Calculating the examples we have

$$\bar{X}_1 = \frac{10 + 10 + 10 + 10 + 10}{5} = \frac{50}{5} = 10,$$

$$s_1 = \sqrt{\frac{(10-10)^2 + (10-10)^2 + (10-10)^2 + (10-10)^2 + (10-10)^2}{5-1}}$$

$$= \sqrt{\frac{0 + 0 + 0 + 0 + 0}{4}}$$

$$s_1 = 0, \text{ and}$$

$$\bar{X}_2 = \frac{0 + 5 + 10 + 15 + 20}{5} = \frac{50}{5} = 10,$$

$$s_2 = \sqrt{\frac{(0-10)^2 + (5-10)^2 + (10-10)^2 + (15-10)^2 + (20-10)^2}{5-1}}$$

$$= \sqrt{\frac{(-10)^2 + (-5)^2 + (0)^2 + (+5)^2 + (+10)^2}{4}}$$

$$= \sqrt{\frac{250}{4}} = \sqrt{62.5}$$

$$s_2 = 7.87.$$

and reference these will be listed before being more fully discussed.

I. Properties of artifacts
  A. Physical
    1. Size
      a. length
      b. width
      c. thickness
      d. platform thickness
    2. Form
      a. flake angle
      b. edge angle
      c. shape
      d. pattern
    3. Material
      a. strength
      b. texture
      c. elemental composition
  B. Conceptual
    1. Mechanical
      a. technological
      b. functional
    2. Stylistic
II. Properties of sites
  A. Physical
    1. Size
      a. area
      b. stratigraphy
    2. Content
      a. specimen distribution
      b. specimen density
    3. Context
      a. location
      b. topography
      c. environment
  B. Conceptual
    1. Ecological
      a. resource strategies
      b. roles
      c. territory
    2. Social
      a. groups
      b. distance
      c. interaction
    3. Demographic

The physical properties of artifacts (IA) and of sites (IIA) are directly observable; they are also directly measurable—even if elaborate apparatus may be necessary to effect the measurements (as is the case for elemental composition). The constituent characteristics of these properties will be treated as variables if they are measured quantitatively, as attributes if qualitatively. The variables which pertain to artifacts are defined in the following manner. (Refer to Figs. 5.1–5.5 for the locations of the artifact landmarks that are mentioned in the definitions.)

Variables of size:

Length (L)   longitudinal dimension from the impact point to the distal edge measured along the medial axis (Fig. 5.2).

Width (W)   maximum lateral dimension measured perpendicular to the medial axis (Fig. 5.2).

Thickness (T)   maximum transverse dimension measured below the bulb of percussion (Fig. 5.2).

Platform Thickness (P_t)   transverse dimension of the platform remnant measured at the impact point (Fig. 5.2).

Variables of form:

Flake angle (β)   the angle between the platform and the ventral face of a specimen (Fig. 5.2).

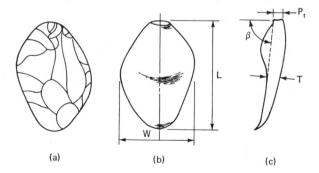

(a)   (b)   (c)

Fig. 5.2

Dimensions of flakes: (a) dorsal face; (b) ventral face view showing relations of length (L) and width (W) to the medial axis; (c) side view showing position of measurements of thickness (T), platform thickness (P_t), and flake angle (β).

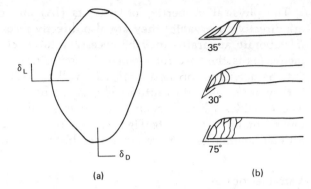

(a)   (b)

Fig. 5.3

Edge angle measurements; (a) locations of lateral (δ_L)
and distal (δ_D) edges; (b) edges of different forms
with angle values noted.

Edge angle (δ)   the angle between the dorsal (back) and
ventral (front) surfaces measured at the
edges of a specimen: δ_L is measured on the
lateral edge; δ_D on the distal edge (Fig. 5.3).

Pattern   the density (measured in number of scars per centi-
meter) and orientation (measured in degrees) of surface scars. Applicable only to points and channel
flakes (Fig. 5.4).

Variables of material:

Strength   the ability of a material to withstand externally
applied loads.

Elemental composition (E)   the chemical trace elements contained in cherts (measured in
parts per million [ppm] by a
technique called neutron activation analysis).

The artifact attributes are defined as follows:

Attributes of form:

Shape   the outline and longitudinal cross-section of a specimen. For specimens other than points, the appropriate measures are for positions of maximum width
and of thickness. For points, a series of shape measures are given in Fig. 5.5.

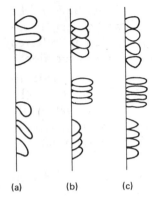

Fig. 5.4

Patterns of retouch scars; (a) direction: normal to edge at top, oblique below; (b) lapped order; (c) ranked order. In all cases, upper scars are expanding, middle scars are parallel, lower scars are contracting.

(a)   (b)   (c)

Attributes of material:

Texture   the relative fineness of the crystalline structure of chert; three arbitrarily chosen categories—from less to more grainy—are used: chalcedony, jasper, quartzite.

The variables and attributes of IA are characteristics of individual specimens; values for each must be treated collectively if they are to be considered in terms of the conceptual properties of IIA. The summary statistics introduced above will be used for this purpose.

The conceptual properties of artifacts are defined:

Mechanical   functions of the laws of physics which pertain to the fracture of brittle, glassy materials such as chert. The magnitude and direction of force ap-

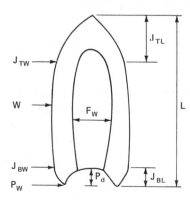

Fig. 5.5

Shape measurements for projectile points. $L = length$, $J_{TL} = tip\ length$, $J_{BL} = base\ length$, $J_{TW} = tip\ width$, $W = width\ at\ midpoint$, $J_{BW} = base\ width$, $P_w = basal\ width$, $P_d = basal\ depth$.

plied in the production of artifacts and in the subsequent use of specimens are of major importance. The processes of production are referred to as technological and those of use as functional.

Stylistic   presumed to be related to processes of social partitioning and group identification. Theory underlying the study of social variation in artifacts is as yet poorly developed, and we will be limited to offering hypotheses rather than conclusions about this variation.

The variables associated with sites are all of size and content.

Variables of size:

Area (A)   that portion of the excavated area which contains 90 percent of material scatter and/or all excavated squares that contain more than 5 specimens per square meter; area is measured in square meters (m²). This restriction is imposed in order to standardize spatial distribution and to compensate for random scatter of materials around living units.

Variables of content:

Distribution   measure of physical distances between specimens of different categories.

Density   number of specimens in a square meter.

Variables of context:

Location   vector distances between a site and other points in geographic space, measured in kilometers (km). Location may also be treated as an attribute if locational points are measured in terms of a set of boundaries rather than in linear distances.

Definitions of site attributes follow.

Attributes of size:

Stratigraphy   layered superposition of different geological materials such as soil, sand, gravel, and so forth.

Attributes of context:

Topography   landform of a part of geographic space.

Environment   conditions existing in a region due to natural

forces—temperature, moisture balance, mineral composition of rocks and soils, animal
and plant communities, as well as many others.   *69*

*An Application
of the Method*

The conceptual properties of sites are defined.

Ecological:

Resource strategy   routinely employed means for obtaining
food and raw material from the environ-
ment.

Role   prescribed form of conduct for participating in a resource strategy.

Territory   unit of land associated with, but not necessarily
exclusively used by a particular group. Its principal function is to divide resources among groups.

Social:

Group   relatively stable set of people who regularly associate
with each other.

Distance   measure of the degree of social separation between
individuals or groups.

Interaction   exchange between groups. The things exchanged
may include raw materials, artifacts, food, personnel, and obligations.

As for demography, we will only refer to some requirements
for maintaining stable populations as these affect other aspects
of hunter-gatherer organization.

LIMITATIONS

Aside from a few pieces of mineral pigments and one small
piece of fossil resin, all the unit assemblages are made up of
chert artifacts and bone debris. Large amounts of more perish-
able materials (such as wood and rawhide) are obviously missing, but their loss will not seriously effect our understanding of
the site. It would be rewarding to know the details of appearance of objects made from these materials. Even without this
knowledge, however, we can infer much. For example, the
presence of jackrabbit bones implies the use of nets for trapping
these animals or of snares for catching them. In either case,
wooden stakes and fiber cordage were probably employed. Additional information about these items would be a welcome addi-

tion to a description of the site, but the absence of this information will not effect the analysis that follows.

More serious limitations are imposed by missing data than by missing information. To reiterate the distinction between data and observations made earlier: observations are made through the direct sense-perception of phenomena; data are abstracted from observations. It is important to remember this distinction in the following discussion. In Roberts' field notes, the information exists that charcoal was scattered over many square meters in several parts of the site. But there is no way to determine the locations of any hearths that may have been associated with these scatters. Consider the following: Distances between hearths are data pertinant to questions about social spacing and may be applied to hypotheses about the spatial organization of camp units. However, unless a way can be found to convert observations about scatter to spacing data, this information can be no more than marginally descriptive for organizational problems. Such data cannot be extracted from the information given, and, thus, more severe limitations are imposed upon questions that may be asked about organization than is desirable.

Another limitation to the spatial analysis is implied in the foregoing discussions of stratigraphy and site units. Locational information is given for almost all specimens recovered during the excavations. Excellent data for investigating variation in artifact characteristics may be extracted from this information. Since these locations are not always clearly associated with stratigraphic levels, however, many specimens cannot be assigned to specific site units. Consequently, the data for investigating interunit variation will in some cases be reduced, and compensations will have to be made in the analysis.

Similarly, a great deal of information about the distribution of bones is given in the field notes, but skeletal parts are seldom specified. Again, the proportional distributions of particular bones with respect to each other are valuable data in relation to questions about social interaction that may be associated with the sharing of animal carcasses. These data, hence these questions, are unavailable to us.

Despite the limitations just innumerated, data pertinent to many questions about the organization of the people who occupied Lindenmeier are obtainable. If we wish to understand something about this organization we must be able to connect the terms specified above to the observable remains of the site. We will make this connection in the form of a model that will have the conceptual properties of sites as primary terms.

In order to construct a model, it is necessary to make some basic assumptions about the universe to which it applies. The purpose of these assumptions is both to simplify the model and to establish the ground rules within which it can operate. We will need to make only four assumptions:

1. Those procurement strategies which are most consistently effective will be most likely to be employed.
2. All food products and raw materials are obtained from wild plant and animal sources and from unaltered, natural mineral deposits.
3. The principal distinctions between members of a group are made on the basis of sex and age.
4. The primary forms of social affiliation are ascribed; they include rules for establishing kinship, residence, and similar associations.

The model first associates resource strategies with locations and territories; next, it links social groups to these; it then specifies the expected interactions between groups.

Figure 5.6 graphically describes the relation between resource strategies, locations, and territories. For stable resources (such as plants), the most efficient spacing of locations within a territory allots an equal but nearby and limited set of resources to each of a number of small locations. However, a central location which incorporates all the smaller units is more efficient than dispersion when resources are scattered and moving (as are herds of large animals). According to this part of the model, stable foods are exploited by groups of minimal size. When a population is primarily dependent upon this type of resource, its members should be fairly evenly dispersed over all its territory; residence units would be the smallest that the organizational structure allows. Conversely, major dependence upon migratory herding species should be accompanied by group concentration in one or a few large residence units.

Most environments offer combinations of stable and mobile foods. Mixed strategies designed to exploit both achieve a balance between the contrasting poles of efficiency associated with each. They also allow a group to concentrate on those foods that are most available at a particular time. If this part of the model is valid, there will be few large sites and many small ones in any hunting-gathering system.

Implied in the resource-dispersion relations just discussed is

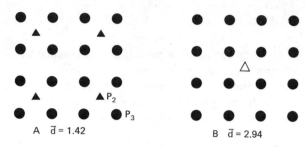

Stable Food

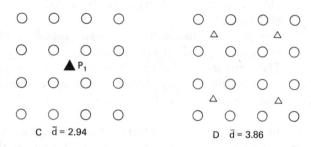

Mobile Food

Fig. 5.6

Distribution of locations as a function of different food procurement strategies. In A and D, locations are dispersed: from each, only immediately adjacent resource points are exploited. In B and C, locations are centralized; from each, all resource points are exploited.

● *points at which predictably stable food resources are located.*

○ *points at which uncertain mobile food resources are located (these points are not all filled simultaneously).*

▲ *most advantageous user location.*

△ *disadvantageous user location.*

P₁ *largest group.*

P₂ *intermediate group.*

P₃ *temporary gathering group.*

d̄ *average procurement effort; the smaller its value, the more efficient a location distribution.*

(*By permission of the* Journal of Anthropological Research.)

the notion that locations and territories should be regularly spaced. Territorial divisions exist to distribute essential resources to all segments of a population. Functionally equivalent locations should be associated with spatial divisions that encompass roughly equivalent resources. For example, the High Plains were occupied, during the nineteenth century, by a number of different bison-hunting tribes. In the vicinity of Lindenmeier, groups of Arapaho, Cheyenne, Shoshone, and Crow maintained territories. Figure 5.7 shows how the dispersion pattern of Fig. 5.6 can be superimposed on various geometric forms of areal division. If spacing regularity is characteristic of hunting societies, then the number of contiguous neighbors for each group will be approximately equal.

The relationship between locations and group sizes should also be regular. The number of persons at a location is dependent upon the functional requirements for implementing a resource strategy at that place. A particular bison-hunting strategy will require a similar number of people—filling the roles of hunter, butcher, shaman, etc.—wherever it is employed. Similarly, seed gathering is best done by a group of fairly constant size. Equivalent places would have the same resident group sizes and larger locations would be combinations of smaller ones.

Finally, the interaction between groups should increase proportionally with increases in the sizes of interacting groups and decrease as the social distance between them becomes greater. Social distance may be measured by counting the number of territorial boundaries intervening between locations. Interactions across boundaries should be less than those within a territory, but interaction rates between equivalent locations that are equally distant should be constant. Among the Plains tribes just mentioned, exchange and communication between the Arapaho and Cheyenne, for example, was much greater than that between the Arapaho and Shoshone.

THE DATA

The following graphs (Figs. 5.8–5.14) describe the distribution of values for each variable measured on artifacts other than projectile points. Each graph is accompanied by a tabulation of the summary statistics for the appropriate variable (Tables 5.1–5.7). The data are pooled separately for each of the occupation units (A, B, F, G, H) with which we are concerned.

As the figures clearly show, all linear measurements—those of length, width, thickness, and platform thickness—are unimodally distributed; that is, the measurements tend to cluster around a few consecutive values. This is strong support for the supposition that we are dealing with a single population of artifact sizes.

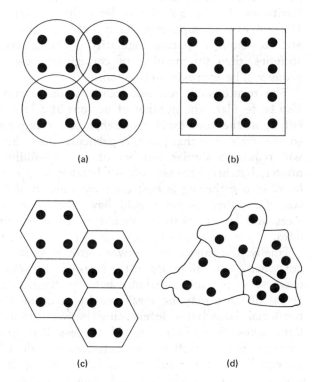

Fig. 5.7

Different ways of dividing space into territories in such a way that all units contain an equal set of resource points: (a) Circles are geometrically most efficient but overlap extensively and leave empty spaces. (b) Squares do not have these disadvantages but increase distances to corners. (c) Hexagons provide the best geometrical compromise. (d) The actual boundaries of the tribes living in the Lindenmeier region during the mid-nineteenth century are shown here in order to contrast hypothetical forms with an empirical case; the distribution of resource points is arbitary.

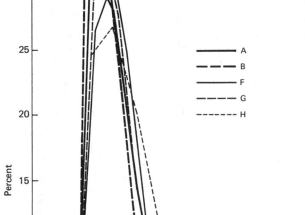

Fig. 5.8

Proportional frequency of specimen length values (L).

Table 5.1
Summary Statistics for Length.

Unit	A	B	F	G	H
$\bar{X}$	33.7	28.5	32.9	32.4	33.4
s	16.0	12.3	14.2	13.0	15.0
N	519	993	173	158	184

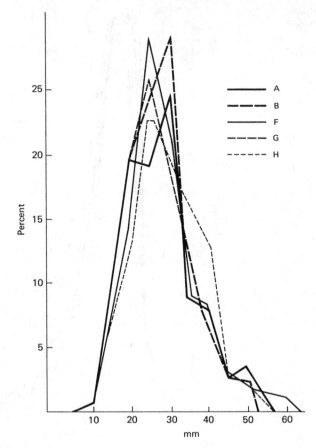

Fig. 5.9

Proportional frequency of specimen width values (W).

Table 5.2
Summary Statistics for Width.

Unit	A	B	F	G	H
$\bar{X}$	27.4	26.3	26.5	26.6	27.4
s	11.5	10.0	8.7	8.2	8.6
N	518	993	173	158	184

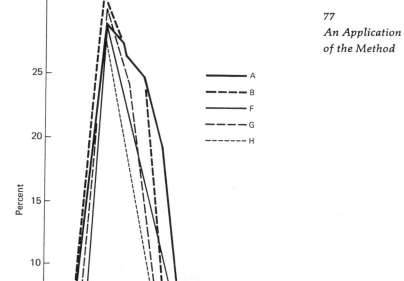

Fig. 5.10

Proportional frequency of thickness values (T).

Table 5.3
Summary Statistics for Thickness.

Unit	A	B	F	G	H
$\overline{X}$	6.3	5.4	5.4	6.2	6.1
s	3.3	3.3	2.5	2.6	3.6
N	519	991	173	158	184

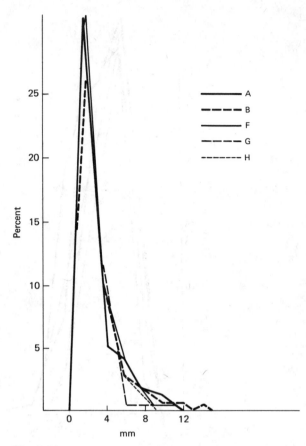

Fig. 5.11

Proportional frequency of specimen platform thickness values (P_t).

Table 5.4
Summary Statistics for Platform Thickness.

Unit	A	B	F	G	H
$\bar{X}$	3.2	2.8	2.3	2.6	2.5
s	2.1	2.0	1.3	1.5	1.7
N	259	433	78	60	76

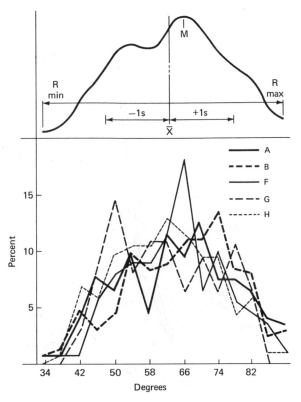

Fig. 5.12

*Proportional frequency of specimen flake angle values
(β). The curve at the top plots the average values for
all five units and shows the positions of the summary
statistics designators.*

Table 5.5
Summary Statistics for Flake Angle.

Unit	A	B	F	G	H
$\overline{X}$	63.6	65.0	63.3	62.3	61.2
s	14.3	13.0	11.3	12.8	12.4
N	227	419	77	59	74

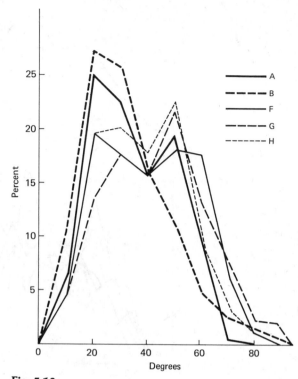

Fig. 5.13

Proportional frequency of specimen lateral edge (δ_L) values. Line legend in Fig. 5.16 applies to Figs. 5.13–5.16.

Table 5.6
Summary Statistics for Lateral Edges.

Unit	A	B	F	G	H
$\bar{X}$	43.9	34.4	38.6	46.0	41.2
s	17.1	16.0	15.3	17.9	15.8
N	383	766	149	136	158

Values of the flake angle are also unimodally distributed but with a wider range of values. This relationship can be more easily seen in the composite, smoothed curve at the top of Fig. 5.12. These values also display a definite clustering tendency, but this is not so pronounced as are those for the linear variables.

The edge angles, δ_L and δ_D, have bimodally distributed values.

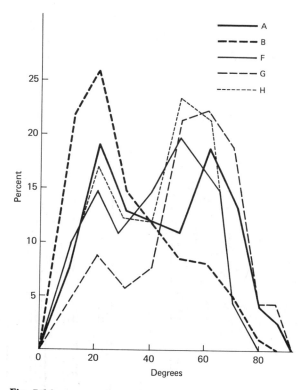

Fig. 5.14

*Proportional frequency of specimen distal edge (δ_D)
values.*

Table 5.7
Summary Statistics for Distal Edges.

Unit	A	B	F	G	H
$\bar{X}$	46.9	34.5	46.3	54.9	44.1
s	20.8	20.8	17.8	19.2	18.1
N	189	396	87	81	87

This may mean that there is more than one factor influencing
the size of these angles.

Figures 5.15 and 5.16 summarize the shape attributes of the
artifacts. These clearly reveal a kind of variation that must have
an underlying selective basis. The kind of materials from which
all specimens, including points and channel flakes, are made is
given in Table 5.8.

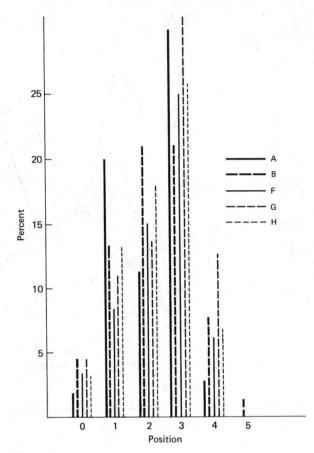

Fig. 5.15

Location of maximum width. 0—proximal end, 1–4 —first through fourth quarter of specimen length, 5—distal end.

Table 5.8

Proportions of Specimens in Each Unit Made from Each Material.

	A	B	F	G	H
Chalcedony	.53	.45	.40	.48	.41
Jasper	.44	.50	.57	.47	.54
Quartzite	.03	.05	.03	.05	.05

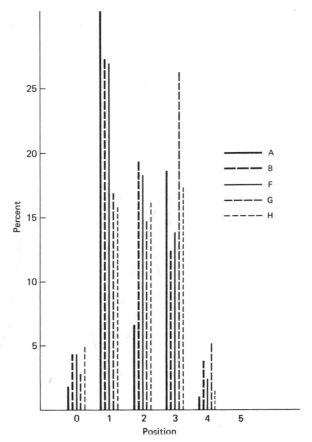

Fig. 5.16

Location of maximum thickness. Intervals same as in
Fig. 5.15.

Table 5.9
Summary Statistics for Variables of Point Size.

	L			W			T		
	N	$\bar{X}$	s	N	$\bar{X}$	s	N	$\bar{X}$	s
A, B	26	35.0	11.3	26	18.3	3.8	26	3.6	0.8
F, G, H	22	31.1	8.4	22	17.8	3.8	22	3.6	0.6

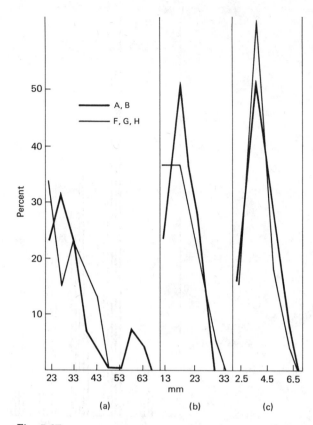

Fig. 5.17

Proportional frequency of point dimension values: (a) length; (b) width at midpoint; (c) thickness. Horizontal scale is in millimeters.

The summary statistics for projectile point variables and attributes are given in Fig. 5.17 and Tables 5.9–5.10. Bearing in mind what was said about the preceding set of data displays it should be possible to draw the appropriate conclusions about the distributions of these values.

We many deduce from the stated propositions of the model that there should be no difference in the artifact content of the occupation units at Lindenmeier if they are socially and functionally equivalent. Alternatively, if they are functionally equivalent but socially distinct, they should differ only in stylistic characteristics or, if socially alike but functionally distinct, only in those mechanical characteristics associated with use.

Table 5.10

Proportional Frequency of Point Pattern Characteristics.

	A, B	F, G, H
Retouch form		
1. expanding	.70	.34
2. parallel	.30	.66
Retouch type		
1. ranked	.24	.66
2. lapped	.76	.34
Retouch direction		
1. perpendicular	.90	0
2. oblique	.10	100

If the variation among all the artifacts in each unit can be accounted for in identical ways, then the hypothesis of no difference will be supported and we will be justified in concluding that all of the Lindenmeier units were occupied at different times by the same group. If, however, differences are detected we must, before examining them for functional or social significance, first ascertain that the observed variation is not due solely to differences in collection procedures during excavation, to measurement errors in the laboratory, or to normal technological variation during the process of artifact production.

6. Analysis

The analysis proceeds through a series of steps designed to test for differences in specified divisions of the data set. The statistical method chosen for most tests is called *one-way analysis of variance*. In it, each variable is examined separately (hence the modifier *one-way*). This method is preferred for the kind of problem being dealt with because the analysis compares all of the measurements of the variable under consideration and calculates a statistic from which to determine whether or not the units into which the data set has been divided differ in that variable. In other words, it examines whether variation within a unit is greater than that among all units. The analysis is repeated for each variable. This chapter will summarize the analytical results without going into the statistical details. Readers interested in a complete account of the procedure should consult the separate monograph on the Lindenmeier site (Wilmsen 1974).

TESTS FOR SITE UNIT DIFFERENCES

The first step must be to determine if the occupation Units A, B, F, G, and H—each taken as a separate entity—differ in any way. Justification for dividing the data set in this way has already been presented in the section on site units, and a hypothesis of no difference has been proposed for the contents of these units.

The results of this first analysis established that the units differ in all variables except width and flake angle. But before drawing conclusions from the results, we must examine the data for any possible inherent bias. In order to be sure that unit differences are not due to differences in materials that might have an effect on flaking characteristics, the proportions of each material texture were calculated and were found to be similar for each unit.

The remaining principal sources of bias are measuring error

and unequal sampling. Measuring error was controlled in the following manner: each of the five students who assisted in gathering the data was given the same four artifacts to measure on several different occasions over a six-month period; during this same period I, too, measured each of these specimens ten times. Means and standard deviations for the set of measurements on each specimen were calculated and average deviations from mean values were computed for each variable. The values for these statistics are displayed in Table 6.1; they are all within the measuring increment for each variable and are uniformly low and consistent between specimens. We may safely conclude that measuring error is negligible.

Sampling inequalities are another matter. Important ways in which sampling bias may contribute to the observed differences between units are implied in the discussion of Roberts' excavation strategies presented in Chapter 3. All artifacts uncovered during the 1934–1936 field seasons were retained in storage but artifact retention was selective in 1938–1940. Retention practices fluctuated in 1937. Now, recall that Unit B was excavated entirely within the 1935–1936 period; its inventory should, accordingly, contain the entire range of stone artifacts that were originally present in that area. Unit A was excavated partly during this period and partly in 1938 while Units F, G, and H were excavated entirely during the 1938–1940 seasons. These latter units should differ markedly in content from Unit B and

Table 6.1

Average Deviations from Means for Four Control Specimens Measured Repeatedly by Six People.

SPEC	L	W	T	P_t	β	δ_L	δ_D
1155	1.16	0.82	0.21	0.14	1.60	4.10	4.00
1164	3.60	1.00	0.20	0.10	1.60	0.70	1.10
1705	0.20	0.20	1.12	0.35	1.70	3.20	—
E425	0.42	0.16	0.61	0.15	1.50	2.30	2.40
$N =$	197	197	197	197	197	177	135
$D =$	0.74mm	0.46mm	0.54mm	0.20mm	1.61°	2.56°	2.74°

$N =$ total number of measurements.

$D =$ combined average deviations for all four specimens. The values are computed by adding the sums of deviations for each specimen and dividing by the total number of observations.

to a lesser extent from Unit A. As the means and standard deviations in Tables 5.1–5.7 show, Unit B is quite clearly the most divergent of the site units. Sampling bias, thus, appears to contribute importantly to unit differences. The recognition of this fact permits us to partition the data set in other ways in order to account for some of the introduced variance.

SOURCES OF VARIATION

In the foregoing section, units for analysis were chosen according to criteria of spatial clustering. Artifact variation that may be independent of location was not considered. If such spatially independent variation can be identified, much of it should be due to the mechanical properties which underlie artifact form. If there is residual variation unexplainable in mechanical terms, it may be examined for stylistic content.

All artifacts are products of some manufacturing process and therefore possess some degree of variation which stems from the technology of their production. By first investigating this component of the total artifact variation, we can account for those variables which are controlled by technological factors, and thus identify simultaneously the number of variables that remain to be explained in other terms.

Technology

In a recent article, Speth (1972) describes the manner in which fracturing takes place in brittle, elastic materials such as chert. When force is applied to these materials in amounts which exceed their breaking strength, spalls are detached in a highly predictable manner. Flaking occurs when the tensile strength of the material is exceeded. In addition to the direction of force application, the important variables in the flaking process are: the distance between the point of impact on the striking platform and the free surface (the core face) from which the spall is detached, and the angle between the planes of the impact and free surfaces (Fig. 6.1). These variables are called, respectively, the platform thickness and the core angle. The core angle is difficult to measure on flakes and is not used in this analysis. The flake angle (β) is presumably related to the impact and core angles, however, and has been used as a measure of technological similarity.

The theory of wave mechanics for glassy materials has been developed entirely for slab-like shapes (such as window panes) in which the impact and free surfaces are parallel to and opposite each other. The kind of spalling that takes place is familiar to everyone who has seen a window struck by a BB-shot or a pebble traveling at high velocity. A spall is dislodged from the surface opposite that hit. The resulting curved depression is created at the points where the tensile strength of the glass is first exceeded by the stress wave originating at the point of impact.

In artifact production, however, impact and free surfaces are adjacent to each other rather than parallel. Nonetheless, the same wave model should account, at least in part, for flake size because there should be a similar relation between the critical variables involved in flake detachment.

Figure 6.1 shows the geometrical relations between these and other pertinent variables; this figure should help you visualize the process just discussed. Both the platform thickness (P_t) and the core angle as well as the direction of force can be controlled in the knapping process; the effects of changes in one upon the others and the consequences for artifact size variation are also diagrammed in this figure. The relationship between variables of flake size and technologically controlled variables is shown in Fig. 6.2; for each increment of decrease in the controlled variables, there is a proportional decrease in flake dimensions. β remains constant. Thus, five (L, W, T, P_t, β) of the seven variables which were measured should be accounted for by technological processes.

It is important to note that these relationships hold only for artifacts that have not been modified by intentional shaping or by use. Consequently, we must extract unmodified flakes from the data set and examine them independently. If the site units are technologically alike, there should be no differences in their unmodified flake characteristics.

Function

Work on functional variation has not reached a level of understanding comparable to that achieved in technological studies. (See Frison 1968 for one of the more interesting functional studies.) Similar mechanical principles of fracture should hold, however, because forces are applied to surfaces of tools. An important difference is that stresses developed during tool use are generally much lower than those involved in flake production. Another difference is that points of force application are at or very near the edges of tools. In this case, shear strength as well as tensile strength is probably critical. Large scale

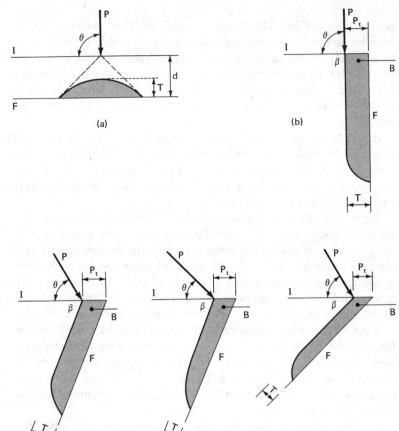

Fig. 6.1

Diagrammatic relations between technological variables effecting the production of flakes.

I	*impact surface (striking platform)*
F	*free surface (core face)*
P	*force*
d	*distance between P and F (equivalent to P_t)*
β	*flake angle*
B	*core angle*
T	*thickness*
shaded area	*detached spall or flake.*

The mechanical spalling model is shown in (a); in (b), this model is transformed to fit the core-flake situation. (c), (d), and (e) show hypothetical flake detachment resulting from different combinations of force directions and core angles.

spalling or flaking should not therefore occur and, in fact, is seldom observed as use wear.

The magnitude of force developed at a working edge depends upon the amount of pressure applied to the tool and upon the hardness of the material with which it is in contact. Although they cannot yet be quantified, the relations between functional force, specimen form, and wear damage may be diagrammed as in Fig. 6.3. In general, damage increases as the hardness of worked material increases and as the angle of application increases. Damage decreases as the size of the working edge increases.

The optimal tool for a task should have edge angles that achieve a compromise between worked material hardness and the ability of the tool material to withstand stress. Chert is many times stronger in compression than in shear or tension; consequently, forces directed into the body of a tool rather than toward a free surface can be absorbed without damage if the amount of tool material at the point of force application is enough to transmit the developed stresses. Tools with edge angles of less than 20° concentrate very little mass along their edges. They are fragile and break under moderate pressure; they were probably seldom used. Edge angles larger than 35° can transmit forces directed straight into the body of the tool without excessive damage but those smaller than 50° break easily under transversely applied loads (see Fig. 6.3a). Edges of 35°–45° are highly efficient for cutting soft materials and for butchering operations. Angles between 50° and 75° have relatively large edge mass concentrations. They are able to absorb heavy shear stresses (Fig. 6.3b). Implements with edges of this size

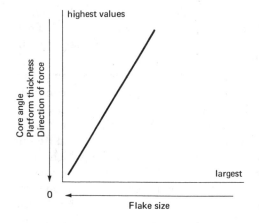

Fig. 6.2

Relationship between controlling technological variables and flake size. (See Fig. 6.1 for key to symbols.)

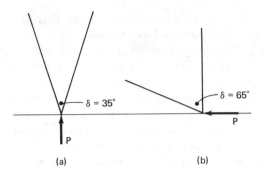

Fig. 6.3

Relationship of functional edge to applied force. P—force, δ—edge angle of tool. Arrow indicates direction of force application; (a) directly into tool; (b) transversely.

are effective for working hard materials. The smaller angles in this range are suitable for cutting bone and wood, the steeper ones for scraping and shaping these materials.

There should be sets of implements with distinctive characteristics that correspond to these different functional requirements. Flakes that have been selected for use but that have not been purposely modified to change their shapes form a distinctive category because the only variation that they should display, in addition to technological variation, should be directly caused by use. Tools have, in addition, a functional component stemming from shape modification. We may, then, divide the remaining artifacts into two categories, utilized flakes and tools. If this division is valid, there should be significant differences between the functional variables of these two categories. They should also be distinguishable from unmodified flakes, but all three categories should be alike technologically.

Functional properties should account for the remaining two variables (δ_D, δ_L) that were measured; however, a complete examination of functional variation would be extremely lengthy. For instance, the category 'tools' might be further investigated for internal variation that can be associated with the different functional tasks mentioned above. The extent to which wear damage varies according to the kinds of functions performed could be considered, and so forth. I will consider only one implication of unit functional differences as an illustration of the directions in which analysis can proceed. Again, additional details are available in the Lindenmeier monograph (Wilmsen 1974). If the units are alike functionally, there should be no differences among them in the categories of tools and utilized flakes. If a unit has smaller edge angles it should also contain other, independent indicators of soft material processing.

Style

Stylistic variation among stone tools is even more poorly understood than is functional variation; it is not even clear to what extent stylistic elements should be present on unifacial tools. For purposes of analysis, style will be defined as the material expression of social distinctions between groups. It will be assumed that the more a specimen is purposefully shaped, the greater will be the potential for social input and, consequently, the greater will be the chance for stylistic elements to be incorporated into that specimen's form.

Take the following examples: (1) If a flake is detached from a core and subsequently left untouched, its entire form will be determined by technological factors. (2) If, instead of being left to lie on the ground, the flake is used to perform some task, it will have a functional as well as a technological component of variation. (3) If, further, the flake is converted by chipping into a tool to make one or more edges regular, those modified edges might contain some stylistic variation. (4) Finally, if the flake is substantially altered so that little of its original form remains, it may have a relatively large stylistic component. Projectile points are among the artifacts that fall into this fourth category. Each category must be examined on its own terms. Figure 6.4

	T	F	S	R
Unmodified flakes	4	0	0	3
Utilized flakes	4	2	0	3
Tools	3	4	2	1
Points	2	4	3	1

Fig. 6.4

Contribution of forming processes to category variance. T—technology, F—function, S—style, R—random. 0—no contribution; 4—most contribution.

diagrams the proportional contributions to category variance attributable to each forming process.

The tool category was examined for stylistic variation and none was found. Patterns of edge retouch and tool shape were considered; they revealed no recognizable regularity other than that attributable to retouch technology. If stylistic elements exist among the unifacial tools, they were not detected by the methods which I employed. Points, however, contain several stylistic indicators; they will be considered separately.

All three of the causative processes that have been postulated —the mechanics of technology and of function and socially controlled style—are subject to random departures from their ideal expressions. Ideal wave mechanics, for example, predicts nothing but ideal flakes; in actuality, however, we seldom find ideal flakes. Random variations occur because of differences in material quality, in the conditions of force application, in individual skill, and other chance factors. Analysis of variance takes randomness into account, and we will not need to be concerned with it except in cases of very small sample size.

CATEGORY VARIATION

Figures 6.5–6.11 display the distributions of values of each variable for the three categories into which the artifacts have been divided—unmodified flakes, utilized flakes, and tools. All of the specimens from all of the units have been lumped together. The tables (6.2–6.8) accompanying the figures tabulate the category means, standard deviations, and ranges for each variable.

There is a great deal of overlap between the categories, just as is expected of categories drawn from the same technological population. But there is also a tendency toward progressively larger sizes and steeper edges among utilized flakes as compared with unmodified flakes. This tendency is even more pronounced among tools. Analysis of variance was performed to test for differences among categories.

Technologically the categories are alike. Platform thickness increases proportionately to specimen size; the flake angle is constant. These results are exactly those predicted by the wave model for a technologically homogeneous set of artifacts.

The categories are functionally distinct. The edges of tools are significantly larger than those of utilized flakes, and these latter are, in turn, significantly larger than those of the unmodified category. Furthermore, unmodified edges fall below the

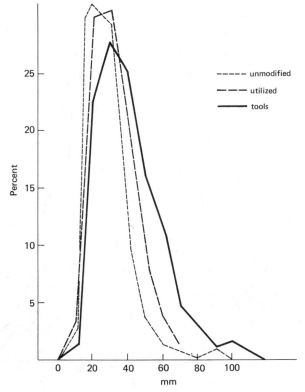

Fig. 6.5

Proportional frequency of category length values (L).

Table 6.2
Summary Statistics for Category Length.

	UNMODIFIED	UTILIZED	TOOLS
$\overline{X}$	26.1	32.8	35.1
s	10.1	14.4	15.3
N	1007	639	1119

limit of usefulness; utilized edges are within the range of maximum cutting effectiveness; and tool edges are within the optimal range for heavy work. Specimen size difference in each category is also significant. Tools are largest; unmodified flakes are smallest.

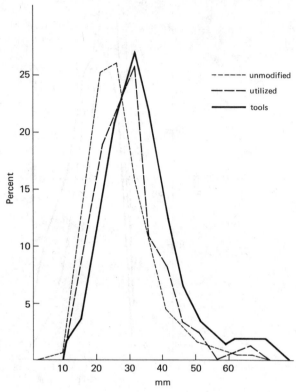

Fig. 6.6

Proportional frequency of category width values (W).

Table 6.3
Summary Statistics for Category Width.

	UNMODIFIED	UTILIZED	TOOLS
$\overline{X}$	24.4	26.8	28.8
s	9.3	10.1	9.8
N	1007	639	1117

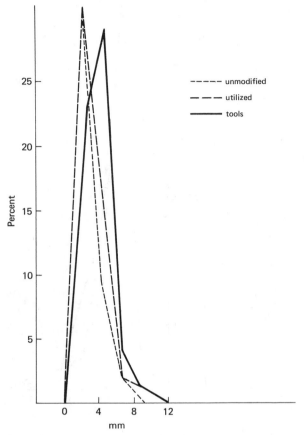

Fig. 6.7

Proportional frequency of category thickness values
(T).

Table 6.4
Summary Statistics for Category Thickness.

	Unmodified	Utilized	Tools
$\bar{X}$	4.8	5.9	6.7
s	2.7	3.9	3.1
N	1006	638	1119

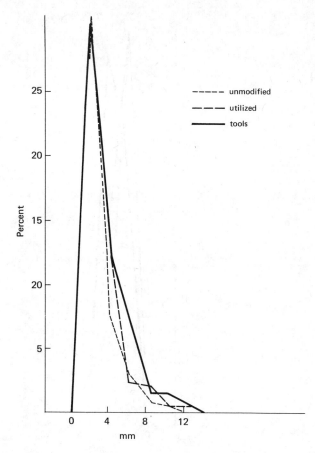

Fig. 6.8

Proportional frequency of category platform thick-ness values (P$_t$).

Table 6.5
Summary Statistics for Category Platform Thickness.

	UNMODIFIED	UTILIZED	TOOLS
$\overline{X}$	2.6	2.9	3.2
s	1.9	2.0	2.1
N	498	319	433

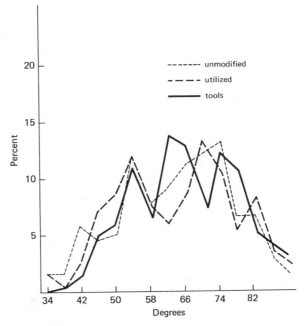

Fig. 6.9

Proportional frequency of category flake angle values (β).

Table 6.6
Summary Statistics for Category Flake Angles.

	UNMODIFIED	UTILIZED	TOOLS
$\bar{X}$	63.3	64.2	64.4
s	13.2	13.7	13.0
N	457	301	408

VARIATION AMONG SITE UNITS

The analysis has supported the hypothesis of functionally distinct but technologically identical categories. We may now re-examine the unit assemblages category by category rather than as undifferentiated sets of artifacts. Recall the hypotheses that will be tested:

1. If the units are technologically alike, there should be no differences in their unmodified flakes. In every unit, we

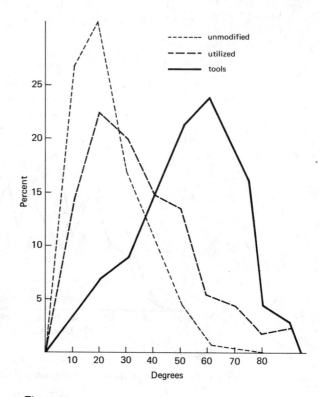

Fig. 6.10

Proportional frequency of category distal angle values
(δ_D).

Table 6.7
Summary Statistics for Category Distal
Angles.

	UNMODIFIED	UTILIZED	TOOLS
$\bar{X}$	25.9	36.6	56.6
s	13.0	19.7	16.7
N	326	228	618

should also expect no differences in the flake angle between
the three categories, and the platform thickness should increase proportionally with specimen size increase.

2. If the units are functionally alike, there should be no differences in their utilized flakes and tools.

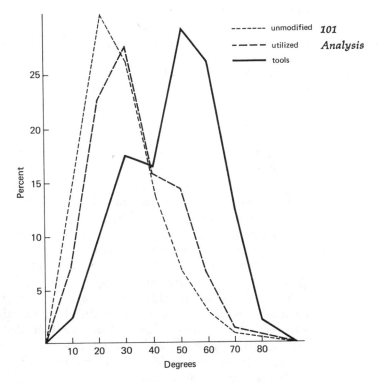

Fig. 6.11

Proportional frequency of category lateral edge values
(δ_L).

Table 6.8
*Summary Statistics for Category Lateral
Angles.*

	Unmodified	Utilized	Tools
$\bar{X}$	30.5	35.8	51.1
s	13.5	15.3	15.4
N	784	500	899

Table 6.9 tabulates the results of the analysis of unmodified
flakes; it also contains the results of platform thickness and
flake angle analysis for the other two categories. The units are
completely alike in technology. Tool platform thickness varies

but in proportion to overall tool size variation. The indeterminacy of utilized flake P_t and β is probably due to randomness in the small sample size. As a check against the possibility that some independent factor (for example, a tendency to break in a certain way) has caused the unmodified category to appear more uniform between areas than it actually is, a separate test was run on unbroken specimens alone. Units A and B were lumped together as were Units F, G, and H in order to make sample sizes as large as possible. The results are presented in Table 6.10; again there is no difference between units.

Utilized flakes are also completely alike as Table 6.11 shows, except that Units F and H have smaller edge angles. But among tools (Table 6.12), there are statistically significant unit differences. Differences in size, although significant, are not great and can be ignored. Edge angles differ by as much as $10°$; this is enough to have clear functional meaning. Again, Unit H has the smallest values, all of them within the predicted range for skin working. Other evidence supports the assignment of skin working functions to this unit. Eleven of twenty-five bone needles found on the site are from Unit H; nine others are from adjacent mixed squares that, in part, contain Unit H material. Needles (see Fig. 6.12) are useful for sewing material such as skins; their presence in large numbers in Unit H lends support to the assignment of a major skin working component in Unit H activities.

Unit A, conversely, has the largest edge angle values; these should be associated with cutting and shaping of bone or wood. Of the 40 bone pieces (Fig. 6.13), other than needles, recovered

Table 6.9

Summary of Analysis of Variance of Unmodified Flakes (all specimens).

	L		W		T		P_t		β	
	N	$\bar{X}$	N	$\bar{X}$	N	$\bar{X}$	N	$\bar{X}$	N	$\bar{X}$
A	197	27.5	197	23.5	197	5.1	107	2.7	86	63.0
B	670	25.3	670	24.8	669	4.8	303	2.7	295	64.2
F	12	24.2	12	21.5	12	3.5	6	1.5	6	60.0
G	7	26.9	7	20.1	7	4.0	1	1.6	1	58.0
H	20	25.5	20	21.3	20	4.0	15	1.7	15	56.1
Signif.	No		No		No		No		No	

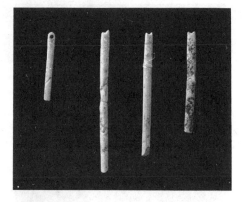

Fig. 6.12

Bone needles with eyes. All are broken; the specimen on the left is 2 mm wide, about the size of a modern bookbinders needle.

from Lindenmeier, 26 were found in Unit A. The unit with the next largest number contained only six.

Unit variation in unifacial artifacts may be summarized in a few words. The initially observed differences were due principally to sampling bias during excavation. Table 6.13 summarizes the proportional differences in unit category content that is the result of this bias. The units were occupied by groups who made their artifacts in the same way and who made the same sets of tools. Functional differences, while probably stemming from different activity emphasis, are variations of degree rather than of kind. Although skin working may have predominated in one place and bone working in another, all of the units contain tools suitable for the entire range of tasks that were necessary to

δ_L		δ_D		$P_{t\ util}$		β_{util}		$P_{t\ tool}$		β_{tool}	
N	$\bar{X}$	N	$\bar{X}$	N	$\bar{X}$	N	$\bar{X}$	N	$\bar{X}$	N	$\bar{X}$
147	32.5	50	28.1	53	2.9	48	59.6	99	3.8	93	66.0
522	30.1	238	25.6	68	3.3	64	66.7	62	2.7	60	66.9
10	23.5	2	17.5	30	2.4	29	65.8	42	2.4	42	62.0
5	31.0	2	30.0	17	2.5	17	66.1	42	2.6	41	60.8
18	30.3	4	20.0	24	1.9	23	57.8	37	3.2	36	65.5
No		No		Indet.		Indet.		Yes		No	

Fig. 6.13

Bone pieces that have been flattened into slab-like forms. The lower, convex edge of c has been incised with a series of short lines. All pieces are broken; a is 94 mm long.

Table 6.10

Summary of Analysis of Variance of Unmodified Flakes (whole, unbroken specimens only).

	L		W		T		P_t	
	N	$\bar{X}$	N	$\bar{X}$	N	$\bar{X}$	N	$\bar{X}$
A, B	302	29.2	302	25.4	301	5.2	212	2.8
F, G, H	23	35.1	23	27.9	23	4.8	20	2.6
Signif.	No		No		No		No	

maintain resident groups. More will be said about the relations between these groups after we have investigated another category of artifacts, projectile points.

VARIATION AMONG POINTS

Folsom points have been mentioned many times throughout this book. I have emphasized them in my illustrations for the same reason that other archaeologists stress them in their analyses. Unlike most other stone artifacts, these and other projectile tips have uniform, usually symmetrical shapes and are thus easy to identify. Every American schoolchild knows how a "spear point" should look; all of us incorporate that abstract category into our conceptual framework when we imagine ourselves to be cowboys on one day and Indians the next.

Their uniformity also sets points aside as a separate analytical category. Modification has altered the original forms of the flakes from which points were made to such an extent that essentially all traces of flake technological variation have been erased. Each step in the manufacturing process (see Fig. 6.14) obscures the characteristics of its predecessor. The few technological traces that remain are mainly associated with fluting; these have been extensively studied by Crabtree (1966) who concludes that most, if not all, Folsom points were made by the same method. Functionally, the points all appear to be equivalent. Substantiation of this statement would require studies of the ballistic and penetrating properties of points, but a point found at Lindenmeier in the neck vertebra of a bison is good inferential evidence that these were effective weapons (Fig. 6.15).

Points obviously cannot yield data relevant to the same ques-

β		δ_L		δ_D	
N	$\bar{X}$	N	$\bar{X}$	N	$\bar{X}$
202	64.4	240	31.3	195	24.9
16	64.4	21	32.4	16	23.8
No		No		No	

Table 6.11

Summary of Analysis of Variance of Utilized Flakes.

	L		W		T		δ_L		δ_D	
	N	$\bar{X}$	N	$\bar{X}$	N	$\bar{X}$	N	$\bar{X}$	N	$\bar{X}$
A	96	35.9	96	28.9	96	6.4	66	41.4	30	35.3
B	146	31.5	146	27.5	145	6.0	107	35.8	63	37.3
F	56	33.5	56	26.7	56	5.1	52	31.3	22	28.4
G	41	35.9	41	27.5	41	6.5	34	36.9	15	39.7
H	61	32.3	61	26.2	61	6.1	48	34.5	21	32.4
Signif.	No		No		No		Yes		No	

Table 6.12

Summary of Analysis of Variance of Tools.

	L		W		T		δ_L		δ_D	
	N	$\bar{X}$	N	$\bar{X}$	N	$\bar{X}$	N	$\bar{X}$	N	$\bar{X}$
A	226	38.2	225	30.1	226	7.4	160	55.7	109	58.8
B	177	37.8	177	31.1	177	7.0	145	47.8	95	54.7
F	105	33.6	105	26.9	105	5.8	86	47.1	63	53.5
G	110	31.4	110	26.7	110	6.3	93	50.9	64	59.2
H	103	35.7	103	29.3	103	6.4	90	45.7	62	49.6
Signif.	Yes		Yes		Yes		Yes		Yes	

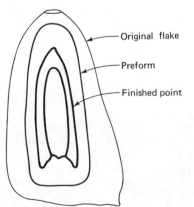

Original flake

Preform

Finished point

Fig. 6.14

Steps in the reduction of a flake to a fluted point. Each succeeding step removes most of its predecessor.

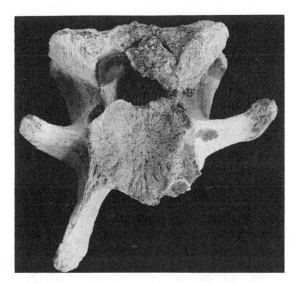

Fig. 6.15

A point embedded in the neural canal of a bison neck vertebra. The lump of material covering the point is consolidated soil, not bone; the point nicked the bone but did not enter it. (By permission of the Smithsonian Institution.)

Table 6.13
Proportions of Artifact Categories in Each Unit. (Unit totals are less than 1.00; points, channel flakes, and bifaces account for the remainder.)

	UNMODIFIED	UTILIZED	TOOLS
A	.38	.18	.36
B	.67	.14	.16
F	.07	.29	.53
G	.04	.23	.63
H	.09	.29	.50

tions for which flakes and tools are ideal subjects. But if social input does increase with increased shaping, points should be the best source of data about social variation. The two assumptions that must be made are: First, that objects such as points are made within the social group that uses them; and second, that increasing degrees of social separation will be accompanied by increasing probabilities that random differences in techniques will become fixed in different groups. If these differences are sufficiently pronounced, they will be measurable on the objects that are made.

Three possible spatial consequences stem from the assumptions: First, if the groups maintain closed boundaries, stylistic elements associated with each will occur in discrete clusters; second, if group boundaries are only partly closed so that some individuals from each may cross to others, stylistic elements will be distributed between areas in proportion to the degree of interaction; and third, if boundaries are completely open, that is, if there is no distinction between groups, stylistic elements will be randomly distributed. I should point out that these are analytical statements of the form "if things are different, those differences should be detectable in predicted ways." Such statements do not explain differences. Note that if we detect stylistic differences between Lindenmeier occupation units, as we shall, we will nonetheless be unable to say what social mechanisms cause these differences. We will only be able to say that some degree of social distance appears to separate the unit groups. Until adequate theory connecting social rules with material variables is developed, we must limit ourselves to inferential interpretations of this kind.

Style differences among Lindenmeier points fit the prediction that different groups were in residence but some interaction took place between them. The data from which this conclusion is drawn are summarized in Figs. 6.16 and 6.17 and in Table 5.10. All units in each area (I and II) were combined in order to increase sample sizes; only whole points were used in the analysis.

Point shapes are distinctively different between areas. Area I points have a rounded outline while those from Area II are straight (Fig. 6.17). Length, width, and thickness are not significantly different; their values are probably closely related to the functional requirements of hafting. Edge retouch form, pattern, and direction differ significantly between the areas but there is some overlap. Tables 6.14 and 6.15 summarize the tests for differences between points in the two areas. Flute flake dorsal scars also have distinctive patterns. We may conclude that two socially distinct groups occupied the Lindenmeier site.

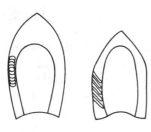

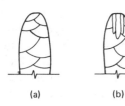

Fig. 6.16

Modal shapes, sizes, and flaking of Units A, B, C points (a) and Units F, G, H points (b). Channel flakes are shown at the bottom of the drawing.

(a)   (b)

Each group appears to have consistently established its campsites in separate locations. We can now look at site units as campsites.

SPATIAL VARIATIONS

Wiessner (1974) has suggested that campsites are structurally related to other organizational components in a hunting society;

(a)   (b)

Fig. 6.17

Projectile points from Area I (Units A, B, C) (a) and Area II (Units F, G, H) (b).

this part of the analysis follows the procedures developed in her paper.

Camp units, regardless of their particular physical forms, should have a regularity and integrity of composition and spacing that is dependent upon the overall settlement strategy of hunters. Within camps, each separate living space—for example, a hut-hearth complex used by a single family—should be similar to other such spaces. Just as artifacts vary according to mechanical and stylistic factors, variations among camps should be a function of ecological and social conditions. Locations at which a number of resource strategies were employed—large animal hunting, plant gathering, and chert collection might be done together—should be structurally different from those at which only a limited number of strategies were activated. These differences will be more pronounced as the number and composition of social groups or as length of time in residence increases. Equivalent camps—those occupied by similar groups for similar reasons—should be alike in composition, size, and layout. Differences among them should be due mainly to chance topographical differences among camp locations.

The artifact composition of the units has already been extensively analyzed. Unit area computations have been given in Table 3.4. Population estimates for each unit may be made by applying the principle of allometric growth to the calculated areas. This principle states that the rate of relative change in one variable (in this case, number of people) is a constant fraction of the rate of change in another (number of square meters). Wiessner has developed a regression curve from which values for either location areas or population sizes of hunting camps may be obtained if the other is known. I have applied the computed areas for Units A, B, F, G, and H to this curve (Fig.

Table 6.14
Summary of t-tests for Significance of Differences Between Area I and Area II Point Variables.

	L		J_{TL}		J_{BL}		J_{TW}	
	N	$\bar{X}$	N	$\bar{X}$	N	$\bar{X}$	N	$\bar{X}$
Area I	26	32.7	23	10.8	25	5.5	24	16.1
Area II	19	31.8	19	12.9	23	5.0	19	16.4
Signif.		No		No		No		No

6.18) and have derived population estimates for the site (Table 6.16). Unit populations are all quite similar. The slight varia-

tions indicated in group sizes could well stem from chance fluctuations in births and deaths of group members. Thus, social group composition and the number of adults available to activate resource strategy roles was probably about the same in each unit.

A method for investigating spatial variation in camp layouts is also given in Wiessner's paper. An outline drawing of each camp is made to the same scale. On this map, the limits of bone scatter and artifact distribution are shown along with hearth and hut locations if these latter are known. The maps are then oriented along the same axis and superimposed upon one another. If the camps have the same basic plan, the parts of each will coincide spatially with their counterparts. Only Units A, B, and F are sufficiently complete to be used with this technique. Figure 6.19 shows the schematic plots of these units separately and superimposed upon each other. These units, and by extension the others, are clearly replicas of a single settlement plan.

Despite differences in orientation imposed by local topography (Units A and B are on opposite sides of a slight ridge and could not have faced the same direction), the basic organization of each unit has been preserved. The relations between bone concentrations and artifact scatter are consistent throughout. The absence of hearth locations in the field notes prevents us from making estimates about individual living units, but it seems reasonable to conclude that all of the units were occupied by equivalently structured groups. The observed variations in plan, though slight, might indicate occupation of some parts of a unit for longer periods of time or reoccupation at different times.

W		J_{BW}		P_W		P_D	
N	$\bar{X}$	N	$\bar{X}$	N	$\bar{X}$	N	$\bar{X}$
26	18.3	22	17.1	21	15.7	23	2.2
19	17.9	16	17.0	16	16.8	17	2.8
	No		No		No		No

Table 6.15

*Proportions of Point Attribute Characteristics for Areas I and II.
Significance Based on X^2 Statistics.*

	RETOUCH FORM		RETOUCH TYPE		RETOUCH DIRECTION	
	EXPAND-ING	PARAL-LEL	RANKED	LAPPED	PERPEN-DICULAR	OBLIQUE
Area I	.63	.37	.24	.76	.90	.10
Area II	.34	.66	.66	.34	0	1.00
Signif.		Yes		Yes		Yes

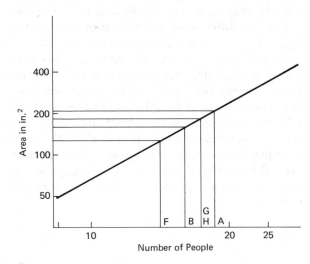

Fig. 6.18

*Relationship of camp area to number of inhabitants
plotted on logarithmic coordinates. The number of
occupants for any area may be found by drawing a
horizontal line from the appropriate point on the
Y-axis until it intersects with the regression curve
and dropping a perpendicular from that point to the
X-axis. The calculations for the five Lindenmeier
units are shown. Verticle (Y) axis—camp area in
yd^2; horizontal (X) axis—number of occupants.*

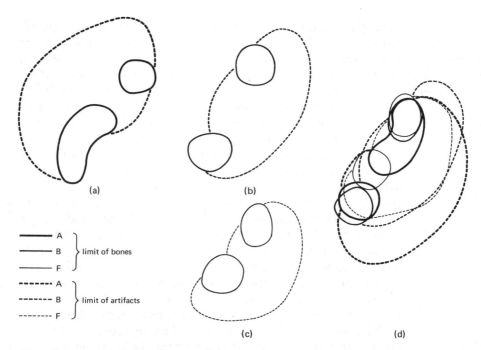

Fig. 6.19

*Schematic plans of units showing similarity of camp layouts: (a) Unit
A; (b) Unit B; (c) Unit F; (d) all three units rotated to the same axis
and superimposed.*

VARIATION IN STONE MATERIAL

All of the stone from which Lindenmeier artifacts were made
was brought to the site; there is no stone in the Lindenmeier
Valley. The location of material sources is, thus, of considerable
interest. Neutron activation analysis is a sensitive technique for
identifying sources; with this technique the proportions of trace

Table 6.16
Estimated Unit Populations (see Fig. 6.18).

	A	B	F	G	H
Area (m²)	179	127	103	166	166
Population	18	14	13	17	17

elements in different materials are calculated and compared. Most sources have distinctive elemental suites and artifacts made from their materials can be identified. The work on Lindenmeier specimens has not yet been completed—it is a slow, expensive process—but preliminary results tend to show differences in proportions of material origins between Areas I and II.

To remain distinct, groups must be apart for substantial periods of time. Furthermore, each probably needs to maintain contact with a somewhat different set of groups. Territorial distinctness and divergent interaction orientations should accompany such a dispersion pattern, and groups should be in contact primarily at those points where their territories intersect. The neutron activation data support the hypothesis that Lindenmeier groups moved in different geographical territories for substantial periods of time. In one of the site areas, exotic raw materials were brought in principally from the north; in the other, imported cherts are mainly of southern origin. This division of areas coincides with the segregation of point styles, and thus the two forms of evidence independently support each other.

The proportion of materials from known sources reinforces the hypothesis as well. Obsidian from Yellowstone Park is found only in Area II while Area I obsidian is from central New Mexico. Both of these sources are about the same distance from Lindenmeier and both are about equally represented in the respective area assemblages. Testing of cherts from 41 other sources is in progress but is not yet complete enough to add to this discussion.

REFERENCES

Frison, George C.
    1968 A functional analysis of certain chipped stone tools. *American Antiquity*, Vol. 33, pp. 149–155.
Speth, John
    1972 Mechanical basis of percussion flaking. *American Antiquity*, Vol. 37, pp. 34–60.
Wiessner, Polly W.
    1974 The use of ethnographic data in archaeological investigation. *American Antiquity*, Vol. 39 (forthcoming).
Wilmsen, Edwin N.
    1974 Lindenmeier: concluding report of investigations, 1934–1972. *Smithsonian Contributions to Anthropology* (forthcoming).

7. Paleo-Indian Band Organization

The Lindenmeier Valley was a frequent camping place for groups of Pleistocene hunters, who came here for many reasons. Animals, providing not only food but materials for clothing and shelters, were to be found in large numbers and in great variety. Water was at least seasonally available. Grass seeds, nuts, and bush fruits undoubtedly grew in profusion and were surely eaten. Other essential resources were easily obtained; chert of excellent quality was present in several nearby places, firewood could be picked up or pruned from trees growing in the valley. And Lindenmeier was an ideal location from which to observe the movements of animals or men over many hundreds of square miles.

But Lindenmeier was not the only advantageous place in the area. Several other equally endowed locations exist today within a few miles of this valley; 11,000 years ago some of these, at least, must also have been as ecologically attractive. It seems unlikely that this place possessed unique environmental properties that made it more desirable than others.

The spatial and social factors that were considered in earlier chapters must have exerted powerful influences upon the selection of this particular valley as a location for recurrent visits. The groups that camped here participated in a single cultural system. They made and used tools in the same way, they set up their campsites in identical fashion, and they appear to have been composed of similar sets of individuals. Group sizes were very much alike, and the differences among these groups were not sufficient to have constituted separate societies. The point-style variations that were found between Areas I and II are no greater than are those between the fastback, loaded-with-extras option of a 1972 car and the basic model of the same brand. We are no more justified in separating the Lindenmeier units into distinct societies than we would be in saying that buyers of the two cars are, necessarily, citizens of different nations. The reasons for the stylistic variations in the two cases are undoubtedly dissimilar, but, in both, they are alternative expressions of a basic theme.

The Lindenmeier groups are most simply explained as member units of a single society. Contact between individuals was sufficiently frequent and strong to maintain intergroup unity. At the same time, social distance between groups must have been great enough to be stylistically expressed over a number of generations. Social distance and spatial distance are reciprocal values and one can be used as an indicator of the other. The fact that point style variates tend to cluster in different parts of the site is evidence that social distinctions were recognized spatially at Lindenmeier.

There appears to have been a social as well as an ecological reason for the occupations in the Lindenmeier Valley. The territorial ranges of two semiautonomous groups probably overlapped here. Periodically, as conditions permitted, these groups scheduled their movements so that they would meet in this valley. They did so to cooperate in bison hunts—which neither probably could carry out alone—and to continue a series of social transactions upon which both depended for continued existence. Mates could be exchanged, adolescents initiated into adulthood, the sick and recently dead given proper ceremonial attention, and the natural environment given whatever ritual care that may have been thought necessary.

The groups need not have remained together for long; a few weeks would have been enough to allow time for all cooperative activities and transactions to be completed. They would then move in their separate directions to exploit other parts of their own territories from other locations. Lindenmeier seems to have been the single largest camp unit in this settlement system, and presumably there were a number of smaller campsites at which fewer people were in temporary residence.

There is at present no way to test these statements. We cannot estimate the duration of site occupation at this or any other open-air site, and we cannot point to any set of locations and say that these belong to a single settlement system. The best that can be said at this moment is that, of the 37 fluted point sites plotted in Fig. 2.1 no more than 2 or 3 approach Lindenmeier in size and complexity. The others are clearly bison- or elephant-kill stations with no indication of other activities. Locations at which only smaller animals or plants were collected have not yet been recognized even though they must have been at least as numerous as the more conspicuous sites where large animals were killed.

Sites with more limited activities should display characteristics appropriate to those activities. Although there are no data for other Folsom sites, some information is available for three Paleo-Indian sites that have other types of points. The Black-water Clovis site was the scene of several bison and elephant kills; the tool assemblage is limited in variety and has the functional characteristics expected ($\bar{X}_{\delta_L} = 48°$). The Horner site in northern Wyoming has yielded the remains of 200 modern bison and a completely predictable tool assemblage ($\bar{X}_{\delta_D} = 54°$, $\bar{X}_{\delta_L} = 45°$). Neither of these sites were camp locations; therefore, populations cannot be estimated. The Levi site in central Texas, on the other hand, is a small rockshelter in which a group of about ten people made a series of short term camps. While there, they quarried and prepared chert and, according to the functional characteristics of the tool assemblage, concentrated on wood or bone implement production ($\bar{X}_{\delta_D} = 67°$, $\bar{X}_{\delta_L} = 55°$).

It should be remembered at this point that the above are only illustrations of the campsite variations that, based on the working model, can be expected in a hunting society's settlement system. Because they are so widely separated in space and time, these sites cannot have been part of a single system and, hence, cannot be called upon to test models of site distribution. They can only provide some indication of the appearance of different kinds of sites. The work of testing a settlement model remains for the future. This will require an intensive survey made over a very large area around Lindenmeier, which presumably will yield no other sites of this size but many kill and gathering locations plus a few moderately large camps.

We must turn to ethnographically known hunting societies for a somewhat fuller picture of band organizational structures in space. The sources from which the following discussion is taken are Burch (1972), Gould (1968), Lee and DeVore (1968), and Steward (1939). Band territories in the Great Basin were distributed in such a way that each spatial unit incorporated several botanical zones; each group was thereby assured equivalent access to important plant resources. Reciprocal hunting rights, however, extended equally to the members of several groups. Camps were regularly established at certain locations and varied in size, duration, and personnel composition according to seasonal and social needs.

!Kung Bushman bands in the Kalahari Desert maintained similar spatial divisions. The rights to use water and plant foods in an area were inherent in group membership but could be shared with relatives and friends. A group had to exercise its rights regularly in order for its claim to be recognized by others. Groups were constantly moving about in their territories and forming camp units with others, but essentially the same set of families formed the core of an interacting unit for long periods of time.

Arctic and subarctic Athabascan and Eskimo bands maintained a similar set of relations between band affiliation, resource allocations, and territories. Again, specific resources and particular locations were key elements in the system.

The gathering of localized plant foods and of small sedentary animals is carried on by minimum household-residence units which function throughout the year. Migratory herding animals are most effectively hunted by several men who assemble at the appropriate season. Bands, thus, are effective structures for implementing multiple resource strategies in order to take advantage of a variety of ecological opportunities. Their most stable identifiable units are the band itself, a fairly large unit of about 20–50 people represented in this study by Lindenmeier; the household-residence unit composed of perhaps two or three families of which the Levi site is an example; and the task-group made up of active adults who perform specific resource roles as at Blackwater and Horner.

Bands incorporate procurement roles in combinations that are most successful for securing an adequate supply of both stable and mobile foods. A balance is achieved between the contrasting tendencies to disperse gathering roles in order to maximize the return from stable resources and to concentrate hunting roles in order to maximize hunting success. But no single resource is uniformly dependable; all are subject to variation in availability and abundance. Band societies are able to recombine resource roles as necessary to meet highly divergent situations without altering their basic organizational plan.

To account for the aggregation of individuals who activate these role positions we must look beyond ecological strategies as such. There are probably many ways in which these roles may be filled; for example, individuals could move at random from band to band momentarily filling appropriate positions. The uncertainties inherent in any such circumstance, the dangers adhering in roles left randomly empty for even short periods must lead, however, to excessive disruption and death in many bands. The existence of many groups would be constantly in jeopardy. Bands, obviously, have evolved ways to overcome these and lesser potential dangers. The stability of band organization rests upon the ability to combine the roles of producer, procreator, associate, and kinsman while permitting individual activation of these roles to fluctuate predictably in response to varying situational conditions.

The immediate daily nutritional and social needs of band members are adequately met in the manner described. But nutritional needs under periodic conditions of extreme scarcity are not. More specifically, demographic requirements for long-term group survival cannot be satisfied by units as small as individual bands. Different and larger units of organization are needed. The ties that bind these larger units together should be more purely social and less directly ecological. Affinal and fictive kinship, ritual sanction, and prestation are among the mechanisms that may be important. Relational terms may be extended to distant fellow bandsmen thereby permitting reciprocal movement of persons between different territorial domains. The area available to each member group for exploitation in times of scarcity is thus many times greater than any single group's territory. The pool of potentially interacting individuals is also greatly increased. (Wilmsen 1973: 25–26.)

Australian Aborigines are recorded to feel direct social and ritual ties with the stone materials originating from their totemic sites. A man sees this stone as part of his own being and carries some of it for use at distant localities within his territorial area even though functionally superior material is locally available. Some of this stone is exchanged between close kinsmen. The exotic stone material at Lindenmeier may well have circulated within a similar network that linked widely dispersed bands.

The model and the methods presented in this book are concerned with understanding the relations between resources, populations, and space in a social system. The ecological components of the model, especially as these are associated with technological and functional variation in artifact assemblages, are reasonably well controlled. The distribution of groups in relation to resources accounts for differences in camp size and composition. Functional variation among artifacts is associated with these differences. Most important for archaeology is the fact that spatial organizations, and their associated social structures, may be deduced when only parts of their systems are visible in the archaeological record.

I will end by returning to the question of origins. Groups that are moving out to colonize unoccupied space will be exposed to fluctuations in resources at least as often as will those which have long been stationary. An organization that ties them to parent groups and a mechanism for continuing the bond between them will be particularly advantageous to the colonizers. Understanding the structure of this organization will enable us to understand the processes of movement in space. Whether the process began in one place or another—whether it began in one place at all—becomes of secondary importance. I have attempted to outline an archaeological approach to these social-geographical phenomena. The next steps in my studies will be to investigate, first, the interrelations between man as predator and the species upon which he preys and, next, the expansion of human groups in space.

REFERENCES

Burch, Ernest S., Jr.
   1972   The caribou/wild reindeer as a human resource. *American Antiquity,* Vol. 37, pp. 339–368.
Gould, Richard
   1968   Living archaeology: the Ngatatjara of western Australia. *Southwestern Journal of Anthropology,* Vol. 24, pp. 101–122.
Lee, Richard B., and Irven DeVore (eds.)
   1968   *Man the Hunter.* Chicago, Aldine.
Steward, Julian H.
   1938   Basin-plateau aboriginal sociopolitical groups. *Bureau of American Ethnology, Bulletin* 120.
Wilmsen, Edwin N.
   1973   Interaction, spacing behavior, and the organization of hunting bands. *Journal of Anthropological Research,* Vol. 29, pp. 25–26.

Glossary

Arroyo: *A steep-sided stream bed or gulch that is usually dry except after heavy rains.*

Assemblage: *All the artifacts found in a given layer at a site.*

Attribute: *An observable feature.*

Band: *A type of society characterized by its small size (usually fewer than 50 people) and integrated primarily by kinship.*

Chert: *A fine-grain rock, glasslike with a conchoidal fracture, light in color.*

Clovis Point: *A distinctive lanceolate spear point characterized by basal thinning achieved by the removal of several flakes or flutes on one or both faces of the point and dating from the late Pleistocene.*

Core: *Nodule of stone from which flakes have been detached.*

Deduction: *A process of reasoning in which a conclusion follows necessarily from the premises presented so that the conclusion cannot be false if the premises are true.*

Fluted Point: *Projectile point characterized by the removal of flakes on one or both faces resulting in a thinning of the base or medial portion of the point.*

Folsom Point: *A distinctive spear point, lanceolate in shape, concave base with broad channel flakes or flutes removed on both faces dating from the late Pleistocene and found in western North America.*

Habitat: *That portion of the environment where a plant or animal naturally occurs.*

Induction: *A process of reasoning in which the conclusion, though supported by the premises, does not follow from them necessarily.*

Industry: *A type of assemblage found time and again in a given region at a given time.*

In situ: *Latin words meaning on the spot, undisturbed.*

Midden: *Refuse heap.*

Neolithic: *Ensemble of postglacial cultures characterized by agriculture, pottery, polished stone tools, and villages. Some of these features may be absent.*

Obsidian: *A volcanic glass, dark in color with a conchoidal fracture.*

Paleo-Indian: *Hunting peoples in the Americas during the late Pleistocene.*

Paleolithic: *Ensemble of prehistoric hunting and gathering cultures characterized by a nonsedentary lifeway and dating from the Pleistocene.*

Pleistocene: *"Ice Age," began at least 2 million years ago and ended about 10 thousand years ago with the Wisconsin glaciation in North America.*

Radiocarbon dating: *A method of absolute dating based on the radioactivity of an isotope of carbon (carbon 14) formed in the atmosphere by cosmic ray action and assimilated by plants at the same time as normal carbon (carbon 12). It passes then to herbivores and carnivores and can be found in their flesh and bones. After the death of the animal or plant no more C-14 is added, and since this C-14 decays by radioactivity at a constant rate, datation is possible.*

Retouch: *The shaping of a tool (from a flake or blade) by removing small secondary flakes either by percussion or by pressure; also, the trace of the small flakes taken off in this fashion.*

Sampling bias: *Error introduced by the investigator, either consciously or unconsciously, in the selecting of samples so that all members in the population to be sampled do not have an equal chance of being selected.*

Stratigraphy: *The study of the deposition of geological layers; also, their order of deposition.*

INDEX

74 75 76 77 9 8 7 6 5 4 3 2 1